Women's Fashions · · · Jewelry · · · Fabrics and Yarns · · · Everything for Kids · · · Wall Coverings · · · Appliances

THE BEST FOR LESS

LYDIA CHERNIAKOVA

A FIRESIDE BOOK

PUBLISHED BY SIMON & SCHUSTER INC.

NEW YORK   LONDON   TORONTO   SYDNEY   TOKYO   SINGAPORE

Men's Clothing · · · Fashion Accessories · · · Underwear and Lingerie · · · Furs · · · Shoes for Men and Women · · · Luggage

Fireside
Simon & Schuster Building
Rockefeller Center
1230 Avenue of the Americas
New York, New York 10020

Designed by Hedgerow Design
Manufactured in the United States of America

1   3   5   7   9   10   8   6   4   2

Library of Congress Cataloging in Publication Data
Cherniakova, Lydia.
The best for less/Lydia Cherniakova.
p.   cm.
"A Fireside book."
1. Shopping—New York (N.Y.)—Guidebooks.   2. New York (N.Y.)—
Description—1981—Guidebooks.   3. Manhattan (New York, N.Y.)—
Description—Guidebooks.   I. Title.
TX336.5.N482N4725   1991
381.45'0002947471—dc20   90-46869
CIP

ISBN 0-671-69370-0

ACKNOWLEDGMENTS

I could not have written this book without a lot of generous help from experts and other friends.

Thanks to Rose Gilbert for moral support and writing expertise and to Ann Preston for being there when the pressure got hard to take.

Andrew Kozin taught me how to judge tailoring and Sandy Bly showed me the quality points on furs. Margaret Lee introduced me to Chinatown shopping and Ely Nack taught me what I know about watches. Richard di Domenico explained how the discount furniture business works, Robert Oppenheim helped with the information on free beauty services, and Mark Russ Federman taught me about caviar and smoked fish. Many other merchants took time out from their busy days to add to my own expertise. My thanks to them all.

CONTENTS

CONTENTS

8

FOREWORD

Shop till I drop? Not me! Not born to shop, either. I don't pass up the art, the architecture, or the cuisine to hit the stores, but eventually I snoop around off the beaten path, to find the best bargains, wherever I am. Shopping is fun, and finding a fabulous bargain is like winning at games. But frankly, I would not pass up a great sunset or an evening of really good conversation for any shopping expedition.

Don't get me wrong, I am a consumer. I know that I can have more of the things I want if I can get them for less. The challenge is to find value, sometimes in unexpected places, and to save money without compromising style, quality, or convenience. In Europe, where I grew up, every woman had her list of "good addresses," of little shops in out-of-the-way places, of factories where the friends of Madame X were discreetly accommodated. In this book I am sharing my "good addresses" in New York with you. Use them and you really will save money.

How can some retailers sell things for so much less than the suggested retail price and stay in business? Does it mean that when stores sell at full retail price they are ripping us off? Definitely not. You get what you pay for, but some of what you pay for may not be important to you: elegant stores at posh addresses, soft lighting, display, advertising, special services, and special events cost money and this cost is built into the retail price. There are merchants who run a more spartan operation, pass the savings on to the customer, and still make a fair profit. If you can do without the frills, you don't have to pay for them. If you want to indulge your champagne taste on a beer budget, you usually can.

UNDERSTANDING
THE LABELS :

Look under Calvin Klein in the Manhattan telephone book, and you will find seven listings. Only one is the couture firm you associate with the name. The others are firms that manufacture and distribute jeans, lingerie, cosmetics, coats, and footwear under a license agreement with Calvin Klein which permits them to use the designer's name. A designer may be extensively or only slightly involved in the design of such merchandise and not at all in the production and distribution.

Many famous designers have such agreements with manufacturers. Laura Ashley and Marimekko sheets, made and sold by Cannon and Springs Mills, come to mind as well as Pierre Cardin luggage and others. There is absolutely nothing wrong with such arrangements: a good designer can use his or her talent at many price points and, since his name is his fortune, he is not likely to let it be used on inferior merchandise.

A few times the system has been abused. The late Halston, for instance, signed some agreements concerning his fragrance line. Then, after some complicated events that involved leveraged buyouts and a lot of lawyers, he ended up not owning his own name as a creative designer. Other firms, tempted by offers of instant cash, have allowed their labels to be used on cheaper fashions made especially for sale at a lower price.

The creative bargain hunter should understand how licensing

works: designer outlet shops in a suburban mall, for instance, may or may not be owned by the designer's own firm. The Calvin Klein outlets in Liberty Village and Woodbury Commons, for instance, are owned by the people who make Calvin Klein jeans, so if you expect to find couture there, you will be disappointed.

Some department stores are in trouble, and to stay afloat they are rethinking their merchandising. We can expect to see changes. In the meantime, discount malls are appearing all over the country, perhaps a wave of the future. The shopping is often good in these malls but it is not the same bargain shopping you find in Manhattan, where you can often get personal service, a willingness to order what's not in stock, and a selection from many sources.

Off-price malls in the area:

SECAUCUS, N.J., five minutes from the Lincoln Tunnel, is not a mall, but a complex of outlets in manufacturers' warehouses. Some are large and elegant, but they are far apart and shopping involves a lot of inconvenient driving and parking, with one exception: There is an indoor mall in the complex, called HARMON COVE OUTLET CENTER, ROUTE 3 (201-348-4780). Here you will find outlets for Bally shoes, Tahari fashions, Barbizon lingerie, and a lot more, under one roof. The building also has a fast food court and is accessible by bus from the Journal Square station of the Hudson Tubes. At the time of this writing, bus #2 leaves from platform B2 on the hour, from 9–6 and returns from the outlet center twenty-five minutes after the hour from 10:25–5:25. Call 201-659-8823 to verify the schedule, but be prepared for some insulting answers, unless you are luckier than I was. There is also a direct bus from the Port Authority Bus Terminal in Manhattan, which runs on a limited schedule. Call 201-653-2220 for information.

Some of the other good shopping sources in Secaucus are within easy walking distance of Harmon Cove and only those are described in this book. For a listing of all the stores in the complex, send one dollar and a self-addressed, stamped envelope, to SOC, P.O. BOX 2187, SECAUCUS, NJ 07094.

LIBERTY VILLAGE in Flemington, NJ, and WOODBURY COM-

MONS in Central Valley, NY (New York Thruway Exit 16 and Route 17) are arranged for parking and walking, which is more enjoyable. Both complexes were developed by the same company as attractive villages devoted to outlet shopping. For information on bus tours, one-day trips, driving instructions, etc., call:
WOODBURY COMMONS: 914-928-6840
LIBERTY VILLAGE: 201-782-8550.

Besides Liberty Village, there are about 100 other outlet shops in the pretty old town of Flemington. Stroll by some of them on the main street or ride the San Francisco-style trolley to shops on the highway. It's one dollar a day, you can get off and on as often as you like, and it goes to all the shops. Call 201-782-7740 for a trolley brochure. There are two bed and breakfast inns where you can stay over: JERICA HILL (201-782-8234) and CABBAGE ROSE (201-788-0247).

Lambertville and New Hope, PA, are a few miles away. It is a nice weekend destination, even without bargain shopping, and for shopping it's outstanding.

For a list of stores contact the HUNTERDON COUNTY CHAMBER OF COMMERCE (201-782-5955).

CREDITS AND RETURNS:

In New York City, the law requires that the store's refund policy is known to customers at the time of purchase. It must be stated either on each sales receipt or on a sign that is prominently displayed near the cash register. The policy may be "Final Sale," which means you keep what you bought. It may be a refund within a certain number of days and store credit for a specified time thereafter, or store credit only. It's entirely up to the store, but they are required to state their policy at the time of purchase. For merchandise that has been reduced, the policy is usually "Final Sale," even if that is not the store's usual policy. Returns must be in the original wrapping, with labels and price tags on and the sales receipt in hand. "Return policy" applies when you choose to return something that is in perfect condition because, for reasons of your own, you don't want to keep it. If what you are returning turned out not to be in perfect condition, the store should take it back regardless of policy, because you did not get what you paid for. If something fell apart ten minutes after you threw out the original wrapping and took off the label, you should not be stuck with it and an honest merchant will not expect that.

"Checks accepted" always means that the store will take a check with proper ID. Two credit cards or one credit card and a driver's license are usually acceptable, but again, it's up to the store.

I try to be on the mailing list of every store in the city, so I get invited to their sales. Usually I don't go right away because I expect that things will be reduced again, sometimes more than once. Selection will be smaller then but prices may be below wholesale.

New York is a city that never stops changing. Neigborhoods change character, businesses come and go, and even old established ones disappear from time to time. Sometimes stores are sold and new management changes both the merchandise and the price structure—so it looks like the same old store, but it's not.

A few of the sources described in this book may no longer be at the same address—or no longer in existence—when you read it, and there may be *new* sources which were not in existence when this book was written. You can avoid being disappointed by telephoning before you go. Also ask about hours, credit, and return policies to be sure they have not changed.

The people and businesses described in this book have been selected on merit and have not paid for the privilege in money or any other consideration. Some may even be surprised to find that they are mentioned in a book.

So put on your best walking shoes, bring a roomy bag and some money, know the sizes of all your loved ones, and take a walking tour. You will have a lot of fun!

WALKING
TOURS

Garment Center Walking Tour • • • Garment Center Walking Tour • • • Garment Center Walking Tour • • • Garment Center Walking Tour • • • Garment Center Walking Tour • • • Garment Center Walking Tour • • •

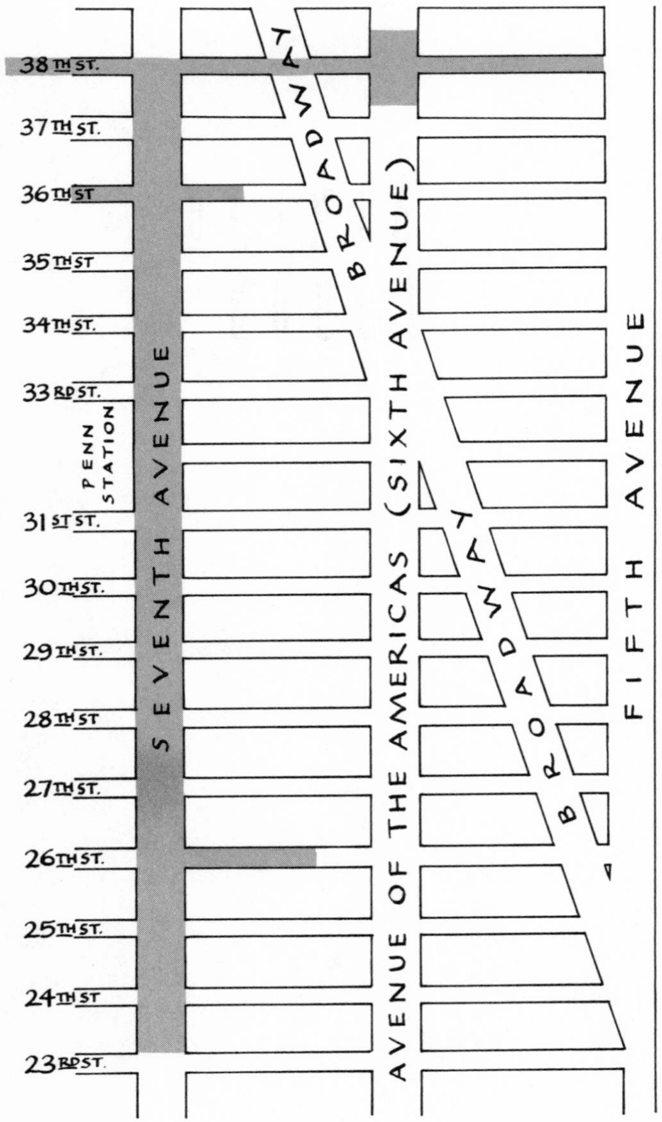

PINS AND
NEEDLES

GARMENT CENTER WALKING TOUR

The neighborhood may look unfashionable, but it is the center of America's fashion industry. Once, long ago, sewing machines were whirring in all the lofts, but now most of the actual cutting and sewing is done elsewhere, for reasons of economy. Designers and sample makers still work in the garment center, and buyers from all over America still come to the showrooms to place their orders. On Broadway and Seventh Avenue, and in the side streets nearby, there are buildings full of showrooms. Occasionally, sample sales are held in these showrooms, to which the public is invited. Everything is sold "as is" and everything is sample size 6, 8, or 10. There are no dressing rooms, all sales are final, and usually only cash is accepted. There are also more comfortable and reliable ways to get bargains in the garment center.

To understand this kind of shopping, one must understand the economics of the garment business: designers and manufacturers can never know which style will suddenly take off and be the best seller of the season, but they must have enough fabric on hand to fill all re-orders, or they will lose business. Often they have made a deal for the exclusive use of a fabric and this commitment can be a huge gamble. If a number becomes a bestseller and they have not enough fabric, they lose orders and money; if, on the other hand, they have too much fabric, buttons, braid, etc., they can cut their losses by offering surplus garments to a discounter at a much smaller profit margin. A good discounter pays at once, and that means a lot in an industry plagued by cash flow problems. Indeed, it is fair to say that manufacturers need to have these discounters standing in the wings. Over the years, they establish firm relationships with each other.

This is why there are a few discreet upstairs sales rooms in the garment center where designer fashions are sold to the public at substantial discounts. These places have sales help and dressing rooms, accept personal checks, and offer a much wider selection than showroom sales.

Some of these firms are also jobbers—middlemen between manufacturers and retailers. They sell to smaller stores and even to big ones, who want only a few pieces of a style. Although some jobbers sell to the public when the public appears at their doorsteps, they don't want to give the appearance of competing with their own customers, the retail stores, so they operate discreetly. Although they carry some of the most fashionable and exclusive designers, when it comes to mentioning these names in print, we are often sworn to silence. Take my word for it: there is hardly a well-known couture line that can not be bought somewhere at a discount of 20 percent or better.

Start the walking tour at Fifth Avenue and Thirty-eighth Street. Lord & Taylor's department store is on this corner and even if you will not shop here today, you can take advantage of their morning hospitality: early-bird customers who arrive before the store opens at 10:00 A.M. are served coffee at the Fifth Avenue entrance.

Window-shop the first floor when the store opens, take the Thirty-eighth Street exit, and you are on Millinery Row. There used to be dozens of street floor milliners on this block, manufacturers who sold to out-of-town retailers and to consumers who walked in off the street, but a number went out of business recently; others have moved upstairs, where rents are more reasonable. If you know where to go, you can still find a selection of hats at good prices. You can also have them made up in the color and material of your choice.

Stop in at the upstairs showroom of:

▶ CARLOS NEW YORK HATS
45 WEST 38 STREET
(869-2207)

The owner-designer is a graduate of the Fashion Institute of Technology (F.I.T.) who learned the finer points of the millinery trade while working for one of the manufacturers who is now out of business. Carlos designs both wearable and outlandish hats (for the Easter Parade, for the theater, etc.). He delivers to stores and boutiques in other parts of the country, but he also sells from stock directly to consumers and does custom work as well. He stocks straw and felt bodies of excellent quality. You can choose from many colors, discuss the trimming, adjust an existing style to fit, with a lower crown, a wider brim, or whatever you want. Don't be put off by the extreme styles you see in the showroom; you can get a nice hat here to wear to work, to lunch, or to church. A simple style will cost between $35 and $50. Very elaborate ones can be as much as $150. *The hours are: 9–5 M–F, 10-3 Sa.*

Carlos is not only talented, he is generous; he suggested that I also look in on a friendly competitor up the street. But first let's visit:

▶ SHERU
49 WEST 38 STREET
(730-0766)

This is a busy, fascinating place where one finds a great variety of merchandise. There are a few reasonably priced hats; all sorts of trimmings: rhinestone and jet braids, buttons, feathers, and flowers; loose beads and the findings to make them into necklaces, metal chains, and a lot more, crammed into every available space and sold at low prices.

The real finds here are in the center showcase, where one can discover very interesting costume jewelry at very low prices: marcasite and Austrian crystal pins, made on the original Victorian and Art Deco molds, really look like precious antiques but cost only $9.50–$15, when I looked last year. Nice cloisonné earrings in Art Deco designs and soft colors were $6 and $7.50. Man-made diamond (cubic zirconia) earrings were $24, African beaded bangles $6. They also have decorative combs and barrettes, necklaces of semiprecious beads, and a great many other things. The stock changes constantly. There even is an ongoing half-price sale in one showcase, which is always full of nice things. If you expect junk at these prices, you will be pleasantly surprised. *The hours here are 10–6 M–F, 9:30–5 Sa.* There is a minimum of $25 for credit card purchases. Refunds are given within two weeks, but there is a 25 percent re-stocking charge.

▶ C I N D E R E L L A
60 WEST 38 STREET
(640-0644)

Despite its name, this business is no stepchild. It is one of the very best sources for silk flowers in the city; the selection is tremendous and the prices wholesale, even if you buy only a single stem.

Since most of the flowers are sold to the millinery trade there are few long stems in the collection, but this can easily be remedied with some of their green wire, leaves, and foliage; buy a flower meant for a hat and transform it into one that can be put in a vase.

Last year imported flowers were priced from $0.70–$4. Handmade silk flowers, made on the premises, cost from $3–$6 per stem, or $30–$80 per dozen. They will even custom-make flowers with your own fabric, so the flower on your hat can match your dress or scarf, but this is pricey: $15–$20 each. Cinderella also sells other supplies: buckram hat bodies, to be covered in fabric;

very dramatic feather boas, from $5–$50; feather trim; veiling and netting; shoulder pads; and all the supplies needed to make one's own bridal headdress. Many brides do just that and save a lot of money.

Open from 8:30–5:15 M–F, 9–4 Sa. All sales are final and for credit card purchases there is a minimum of $30.

▶ M A N N Y ' S
63 WEST 38 STREET
(840-2235)

Always busy, always a little dishevelled, this store supplies the millinery trade as well as individual consumers. There are trimmed and untrimmed hats and all sorts of supplies: ribbons, feathers, flowers, veiling, and a lot more. Prices are among the best in town.

The hours are: 9–5:30 M–F, 9–3:30 Sa. Major credit cards are accepted and all sales are final.

▶ H Y M A N   H E N D L E R
63 WEST 38 STREET
(840-8393)

The most beautiful ribbons can be found here, and usually nowhere else, because they are designed by Mr. Hendler and made in Europe just for him. The garment and millinery trades, American couture houses, upscale out-of-town retailers, and the costume studios of opera and ballet companies are the mainstay of his business, but consumers who come to the store will be accommodated. Some of these ribbons are really works of art and they can be expensive, but half a yard can transform a pedestrian outfit into something fabulous. There are also plenty of ribbons for a dollar or two, as well as tassel fringes for the home and braids for your own Chanel-inspired suits.

The hours are 9–5:30 M–F, closed Saturday. Credit cards are not accepted; personal checks are welcome and all sales are final.

► **M R . W I L L I E**
66 WEST 38 STREET, ROOM 402
(382-1795)

Recommended by Carlos, this is another talented F.I.T. graduate with a lot of imagination. He sometimes gets carried away and designs creations that few of us could wear, but when called upon, he will use his talents to make handsome and wearable hats. Willie, who delivers to many out-of-town boutiques, loves to work with private customers and is very service-oriented. You can select from many colors of straw or felt and Willie's trims are very inventive.

Prices run from $30–$80, depending on the cost of the material and the amount of labor involved, but if you bring this book along, he will give you an additional discount of 15 percent on your first purchase. He sees customers by appointment, but you can stop in and get acquainted on the walking tour.

Now walk to the corner of Sixth Avenue (really Avenue of the Americas, but that name has never been accepted by New Yorkers), and turn left. In the next block you will find:

► **N E W S T A R H A N D B A G S , I N C .**
1010 AVENUE OF THE AMERICAS
(869-4013)

This is one of the very best sources in the city for eelskin items. The prices are excellent. Eelskin is glossy in texture and light in weight, but it wears like iron. Items made of this leather are characterized by a striped effect, because the skins are long and narrow and have to be pieced together.

Men's wallets of eelskin with lots of credit card slots were $19 in a good choice of colors, the day we looked. Small French purses for women were $25, large wallets with two compartments for bills, credit card slots, and a zippered change purse were $39. Small handbags were on sale for $39, larger ones cost $77–$99. There were also great eelskin briefcases with outside pockets and shoulder straps for $149 and $159. I have seen many of these items elsewhere for higher prices.

For evening, there is a big collection of gold- and silver-toned minaudières, the little metal evening boxes with shoulder chains. Some are sculptured shapes, others are trimmed with rhinestones for a very dressy look. Prices range from $40–$100.

The hours here are 10–6 M–Sa, and major credit cards are accepted. All sales are final, so be sure you want to keep what you buy.

▶ M & J TRIMMINGS CO.
1008 AVENUE OF THE AMERICAS
(391-9072)

A large, neat store with the most incredible selection of ribbons, braids, buttons, buckles, laces, and all sorts of other ornaments— anything you could ever imagine and a lot of things you may never have imagined.

The hours are: 9–6 M–F, 10–3 Sa. Major credit cards are accepted and all sales are final.

▶ JOSEPH HERSH
1000 AVENUE OF THE AMERICAS
(391-6615)

One of the few remaining stores in Manhattan that specialize in dressmakers' supplies. Needles, threads, scissors, buttons, elastic, interlining, seam binding, zippers, shoulder pads, and similar items are sold to the public as well as to the trade, and the selection is vast.

The hours are: 9:30–5:30 M, 9–5 Tu–F, 11–4 Sa. There is a $25 minimum for Visa and MasterCard. Store credits are given within seven days of purchase.

Return to 38th Street and continue walking west. You will find:

▶ GORDON BUTTONS
142 WEST 38 STREET
(921-1684)

Check your wardrobe for missing buttons before you come, because there are thousands of buttons of every possible kind here, in hundreds of colors and styles—an absolutely fantastic selection, and prices are very fair. Gordon's premises are shared by:

▶ SERVICE NOTIONS AND TRIMMINGS
142 WEST 38 STREET
(921-1680)

The trade comes here for zippers, thread (on large cones), shoulder pads, and other notions. Some things are sold in quantities consumers can use, others are not. Both establishments accept cash only and all sales are final. *The hours: 8:45–5:30, M–F.*

You are now in the heart of the garment center, where you can shop for designer fashions. Stay on Thirty-eighth Street and walk west, to visit:

▶ IRVING KATZ
209 WEST 38 STREET
(944-7200)

On one side of the elevator is a wholesale showroom where store buyers come to order the firm's superb leather and Ultrasuede fashions; on the other side is a salesroom for consumers. Here you will find current fashions by Adele Simpson, Debra Kushme, St. Gilian, Perry John, and others; mohair coats by Paul Levy; suits by George Symington, and Katz's own elegant leather garments. They use top-quality English lambskin and butter-soft Palova, as well as a soft pigskin in high-fashion colors. They also work in Ultrasuede and Facil, a softer version of Ultrasuede, which drapes beautifully. Average discounts are claimed to be 25–50 percent.

This is also a great source for handbags by Susan Gail and Varon; there is a good selection at excellent prices.

The showroom is closed every year for the first two weeks of July. In June there is a tremendous end-of-season sale and when they reopen the third week of July, the fall merchandise is ready. Sizes are 2–18, but if your size is at either extreme of this scale, call ahead to be sure it's in stock.

The hours are 9–5 M–F; Saturdays they open only during their busy season, so call before you come.

Credit cards are not accepted, but personal checks with ID are welcome. All sales are final.

When you leave here, continue along 38th Street and visit:

▶ **ZYNN FASHIONS**
270 WEST 38 STREET
(944-8686)

Mr. Zynn, the owner, is a master tailor who is also a contractor for some very big names in the fashion world. Contractors produce the garments created and sold by a designer, using the fabrics which the designers specify. If you like that designer's fashions, but they don't fit you, Zynn will make you a coat, jacket, suit, etc. to your own measurements. If it fits off the rack, you can buy it here for less than half the retail price. He can also change a style, copy a favorite garment, or design something just for you, with your own fabric or his. Mr. Zynn calls himself the last of the Mohicans—when he retires, there will be no more tailors who do fine custom work in the garment center. His work is very fine, his prices are reasonable, and the showroom is spartan. His hours are by appointment, he takes checks but no credit cards, and, of course, custom-made clothes cannot be returned.

Now return to Seventh Avenue, turn right, go to Thirty-sixth Street, turn left and look in on two excellent bargain sources in the same building:

▶ A B E   G E L L E R
141 WEST 36 STREET
(736-8077)

A pleasant showroom, presided over by the genial Ms. Edith, who insisted on only one thing when I interviewed her: she does not want her designers' names mentioned in print, because it might get her in trouble with her suppliers. I respect her wishes, but when you come in, you will see some very big names, in current styles. Ask about the famous designer who does imaginative appliqué. I saw lots of dressy styles, as well as designer sportswear, coats, suits, and interesting fun furs. A patchwork rabbit jacket in many dark, vibrant colors, for instance, was $250 last year. Around December 15 and again early in June, there is always a big sale.

Sizes are 4–16, and discounts are claimed to be one third.

The hours are 9–5 M–F, 9–3 Sa, but closed Saturdays from July 15 until Labor Day and closed for vacation the first two weeks in July.

Credit cards are not accepted, but personal checks with ID are welcome. All sales are final—no credits, no refunds.

In the same building is:

▶ S T A N R O S E
141 WEST 36 STREET
(736-3358)

A small selection of really elegant daytime and evening fashions, chosen with taste and flair. Mr. Rose also became nervous when the subject of designers' names came up, and no wonder—I saw couture labels in his showroom that I have seen nowhere else at discount and he wants to protect his sources. All his merchandise is current and discounts are claimed to be 38–60 percent. Sizes are 4–12.

There is a big sale here every December and June, and the place closes for vacaton during the month of July.

The hours are: 9:30–5 M–F, 10–4 Sa. Credit cards are not accepted, but personal checks are welcome. All sales are final.

Return to Seventh Avenue, cross the street to the west side of the avenue, and walk a block and a half to visit:

▶ M S, M I S S O R M R S
462 SEVENTH AVENUE, BETWEEN 34TH AND 35TH STREETS
(736-0557)

This is the retail showroom of Ben Farber, a major jobber in the fashion trade. Despite the company's efforts to keep this showroom separate from its wholesale business by giving it a cute name, almost everybody who shops here calls it Ben Farber. By either name, it's a great place to shop for top fashions at discounts that are claimed to be 20 percent or more.

They work with almost four hundred designer brands and carry daytime and evening dresses, suits, coats, knits, sometimes furs, and high-fashion separates. Styles range from conservative to super-trendy. Bill Blass, Adrienne Vittadini, Julie Francis, Harvé Benard, Drizzle, Tahari, the dressy styles of Raoul Blanco, and others whom I have been asked not to mention in print are sold here. Talented designers who are on their way up often give good value. When one of them suddenly becomes hot, the partners here will add him or her to their collection immediately while the big retailers deliberate.

There is Ultrasuede and Ultraleather, real leather, fur-lined and reversible silk and fur raincoats. At the end of the spring 1989 season I saw a coat that reversed from silk to black opossum reduced to $650, as well as a respectable mink coat with dyed-to-match fox tuxedo, reduced to $1679.

From time to time things go on sale, usually at the end of the season, and there are always a few racks tucked in some corner, where leftover or shop-worn fashions are sold at rock-bottom prices. I have seen silk dresses that retailed for over $500 sold here with small flaws for $9.95.

This is one of the few fashion discounters who carries a wide range of sizes, from 2 to 24, but the more unusual sizes are only available by special order.

Also available by special order is almost any garment from the many manufacturers this firm deals with. You supply the manufacturer's name, the style number, the size, color, and retail price; all this information is available on the hang tag in retail stores. If you are ordering something you have seen in a magazine, they can often track down the style number from a picture. If the garment is not in stock, they will order it for you, if it is still available. Special orders can be placed by phone or in the showroom and a non-refundable 50 percent deposit of Farber's price will confirm the order.

The hours are 9–5:30 M–F, 9–4 Sa, 10–4 Su, except in December, January, June, and July, when the showroom is closed on Sundays.

Credit cards are not accepted, but personal checks are welcome and all sales are final.

There is nothing of much interest on Seventh Avenue between here and Thirtieth Street, except for a row of fast-food restaurants. If you don't want a junk-food fix, take a bus for these few blocks and save your energy for the bargain stores that await you. Get off at Thirtieth Street, the heart of the fur district. You can buy a fur coat here at the wholesale price, but read chapter 8 first. You will need an appointment with a fur manufacturer and time to look around, but today you can stop in at:

▶ A A R O N   W E I N I N G
348 SEVENTH AVENUE
(244-6993)

A high quality street-level source for small furs: hats, scarves, headbands, and all sorts of other fur accessories, made of mink and fox of many colors, of fur that has been dyed in bright hues, and of raccoon, lynx, and other long-haired furs. The skins are of good quality, the styles are elegant, and custom work of all sorts is possible. Try a hat and matching scarf over a cloth coat or suit instead of a fur collar—more dashing and much more versatile. Prices are very reasonable compared to stores on Fifth Avenue. Bring this book along when you shop, and they will give you an additional 10 percent discount.

The hours are 10–4 M–F, Saturday (during the winter season only) 10–2. All sales are final, except by prior arrangement. American Express and Visa cards are accepted.

Next stop:

▶ ## HARRIS COATS AND SUITS
330 SEVENTH AVENUE
(563-0079)

A large showroom, full of cloth coats, suits, raincoats, and, in season, man-made furs. Coats and suits are either Harris's own make—of excellent quality—or brands like Harvé Benard and J. G. Hook. In addition to 100 percent pure wool, you will find cashmere, camel hair, mohair, Ultrasuede, and Ultraleather. Sizes range from 2–24 and if nothing in stock fits, they will make it up just for you, for a small additional charge. Other services include a wool interlining that can be put into any of their coats for $15; it can make a big difference to your comfort level on a cold winter day. Alterations here are free, except on raincoats by London Fog, Misty Harbor, Drizzle, and Count Romy. The manmade fur coats are made by Harris.

There are end-of-season sales every January and May. A private sale of current merchandise, for established customers, starts around Labor Day. At any time you will get an additional 10 percent discount if you bring this book.

The hours are 9–5:30 M–F, 9–4:30 Sa, 9–3:30 Su.

Major credit cards are accepted and store credit given within seven days of purchase.

▶ **P R G**
307 SEVENTH AVENUE
(627-1132)

A well-selected assortment of designer sportswear, dresses, and accessories. These styles are also carried at Bloomingdale's, Saks, and Bergdorf Goodman, but they cost 20 to 50 percent less here. This is PRG's second store; we will come to the original one, on 26th Street, a little later. Both stores are very service-oriented and accept special orders by phone if the customer supplies the style number, size, and color. You will, however, have to come in to see what's carried, because I have been asked not to embarrass these exclusive designers by mentioning their names in print in connection with a discount store. Delivery via UPS is available.

The hours are 10–6:30 M–W, F–Sa, 10–7 Th. Major credit cards are accepted and store credit given within seven days of purchase, but sale items cannot be returned.

▶ **T R U E M A R T   F A B R I C S**
261 SEVENTH AVENUE
(924-1332)

Don't be fooled by the table near the entrance, where fabric remnants are displayed in a heap. That's for the walk-in trade—people who don't know fine fabric when they see it.

The stock for serious customers comes from such illustrious sources as Geoffrey Beene, Calvin Klein, and Perry Ellis and consists of their end-of-season remnants. I saw lots of silks and rayons, wool coating, and menswear suiting from some of the best mills, at true bargain prices. I loved the sheer wool prints and the quilted and printed velvet. The selection is comprehensive and very fashionable; in addition to distinctive patterns and designs I saw staples like black wool jersey and China silk, which are hard to find because couture houses may not dispose of them at the end of the season.

The fabrics are fine, but the operation is basic: you won't find pattern books or notions here. For yardages, zippers, and thread you're on your own.

Students from nearby F.I.T. are constantly in this store in search of fabrics for school projects.

The hours are 12–8 M–Sa. Credit cards and personal checks are not accepted.

S&W is a complex of four stores on and near the corner of 26th Street. The telephone number for all the stores is 924-6656 and discounts in all the stores are claimed to average 20 percent to 30 percent.

During end-of-season sales in January and July, prices are reduced again a minimum of 50 percent. Since they have to accept some of next season's merchandise long before most customers think of shopping, they often have pre-season sales to induce us to shop really early. If you show this book in September, October, April, or May, an extra 10 percent will be taken off the marked price, except on items that are already on sale.

The hours for all stores are 10–6:30 M–F (except 10–8 Th). 10–6 Su. Major credit cards are accepted and store credit or exchanges are given within seven days of purchase.

► S & W   S H O E S   A N D   H A N D B A G S
283 SEVENTH AVENUE

A fashionable collection of imported shoes.

► S & W   C O A T S
287 SEVENTH AVENUE

A good selection of quality cloth coats, including cashmere and other precious fibers, raincoats, leather and shearling coats, as well as fur-lined raincoats are sold here.

► S&W MAIN STORE
165 WEST 26 STREET

Designer sportswear, dresses, and blouses with very good labels.

▶ S & W   OUTLET
170 WEST 26 STREET

Odds and ends from all S&W stores are disposed of here. The merchandise is not always in perfect condition, but the prices are really low. All sales are final and there are no extra discounts if you bring this book.

Other S&W stores are at:

4217 13TH AVENUE, BROOKLYN (718-438-9879)
437 MOUNT PLEASANT AVENUE, LIVINGSTON, NJ
  (201-992-8777)
365 CENTRAL AVENUE, SCARSDALE, NY (914-723-5335)

▶ PRG
160 WEST 26 STREET
(620-0409)

This store is larger than the one around the corner and it is managed by the owners. There is more pricey high fashion here, but you can also find affordable dresses and sportswear at discounts of 20–50 percent. On the accessory counter you may find signature scarves and nice belts.

The hours here are 10–6 Su–F, but 10–7 on Thursdays. Major credit cards are accepted and store credit given within seven days of purchase. Both PRG stores will give an extra 10 percent off on clothes, but not on accessories or sale items, if you bring this book.

The only men's shop on this walking tour is:

▶ E X P L O R E R' S   C O M P A N Y
228 SEVENTH AVE, AT 23RD STREET
(255-4686)

Elegant casual clothes are sold at a claimed discount of 35 to 65 percent. *It's open seven days a week: 11–7 M–F, 11–6 Sa, 12–5 Su.*

Major credit cards are accepted and refunds given within ten days of purchase. For further description and a listing of all the stores in this chain, see chapter 11: Men's Clothing.

If you are ready for a leisurely drink or dinner, go across the street to:

▶ M U L L E N S
233 SEVENTH AVENUE
(255-6611)

This Irish pub has been here for many years and became gentrified with the rest of Chelsea. It's a cozy neighborhood place with a long bar, red tablecloths, hunting prints and candles in the dining room, and friendly waitresses with Irish accents. The food is simple and good: homemade soup, steak, roast chicken, fish filet, and trifle for dessert. The prices are really low and it's a nice place to end your walking tour.

Lower Manhattan Walking Tour

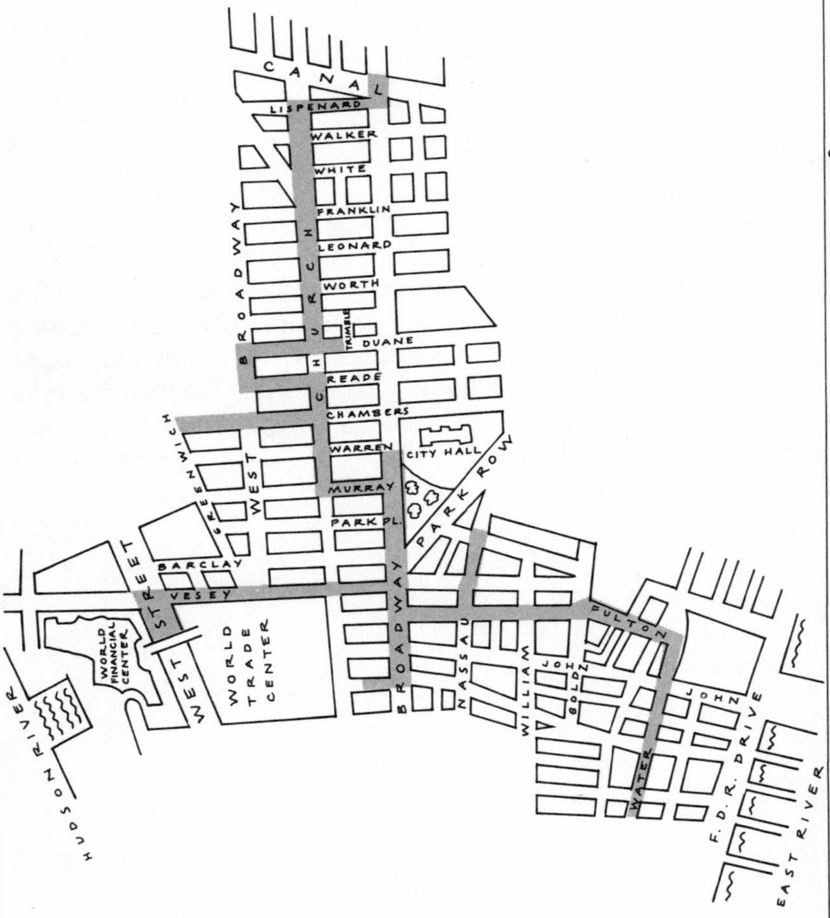

HISTORY AND BARGAINS

LOWER MANHATTAN WALKING TOUR

This tour will take you through a part of New York that would be fascinating even if there were no bargain stores, but the shopping is excellent. Office workers crowd the streets and stores during the week, but on Saturday all is serene, it's the best time to come. You can do the whole tour in one rather long day, or break it up into sections, each will be rewarding in its own way.

Start at Broadway and Canal Street, which you can reach on the Broadway buses #1 or #6, or on the N, R, J, M, Z, or 6 subway trains.

Canal is an interesting street, worthy of a day's exploration on your own, some other time. Today, note only:

▶ TUNNEL STATIONERY
301 CANAL STREET
(431-6330)

All sorts of office and school supplies and a vast assortment of pens are sold at discounts that are claimed to be 15 percent to 30 percent. I have bought manila envelopes here for even less. *Store hours: 7 days a week, 8–5 M–F, 9–5 Sa, Su.*

Their other store,

▶ TUNNEL STATIONERY
414 BROADWAY (AT CANAL STREET)
(431-6663)

sells a selection of greeting cards at claimed discounts of 15 to 30 percent. In addition to well-known cards, there are unusual and offbeat ones and small editions by Soho artists. There are also gift items, stuffed animals, status pens, boxed writing paper, and a good selection of art supplies. Printing is available. Occasionally Christmas cards are 50 percent off in October.

The hours are 9–6 M–Sa, but they may decide to close on Saturday in the summer, so call before you go.

In both stores, credit cards are not accepted; refunds are given within thirty days of purchase.

▶ FABRIC WAREHOUSE
406 BROADWAY
(431-9510)

This is the only fabric store in this book that carries fabrics you would expect in a shopping mall fabric store, but here they are sold at claimed discounts of 20 percent to 50 percent. There are lots of polyesters and blends, corduroys, knits, etc., but no couture imports, and not too many natural fibers. I once made stylish kitchen curtains from a cotton dress fabric that cost $1 a yard here.

The store also carries notions and patterns by Butterick and New Look. *Open seven days a week: 9–7:30 Thu, 9–6 other weekdays, 10–5 Sa, Su.* Visa and MasterCard are accepted, and all sales are final.

Turn right into Lispenard Street, which is two blocks long, and find:

▶ LOUIS BARRALL AND SON
58 LISPENARD STREET
(226-6195)

This old-fashioned-looking men's clothing store with old-fashioned values has been on this block for eighty-five years. They carry conservatively styled suits and raincoats with familiar labels from some of the better manufacturers. Quality and selection are good and prices for first quality (white label) are claimed to be at least one-third off the retail price, often more. Garments with green labels are slightly irregular and the salespeople will point out the flaw that makes them so. Prices of irregulars are claimed to be at least 50 percent off. I saw a group of slacks that usually retails for $95–$165, at $35 each. The stock consists of closeouts, job lots, and cancelled orders, which means that you will find whatever Mr. Barrall has been able to get at the right price. You may not find every style in every size, but the selection is good and when you find what you like in your size, you will really get a bargain. Sizes 37–50 in Regular, Short, and Tall are usually available and Portly or Portly Short are available from time to time.

The hours are: 9:30–6 M–F, 9:30–5 Sa. Refunds are given within two weeks; credit cards are not accepted here, but personal checks are.

Across the street is the rear entrance to:

▶ PEARL PAINT
308 CANAL STREET
(431-7932)

You will find house paint by Benjamin Moore at 20 percent below retail here and a big assortment of artists' supplies at similar or even better discounts; it's a favorite of many Soho artists. Nonartists will find portfolios, diaries, and a really beautiful assortment of pens. Ink for the pens as well as felt tip pens come in more colors than you can imagine, and there is also writing paper in 44 delectable colors. Buy the paper here, take it to your neighborhood print shop, and get beautiful personal stationery for very little.

The store is open seven days a week: 9–5:30 M–Sa, Thu till 7, 11– 5 Su. Visa and MasterCard are accepted. Store credit, but no re- fund, is given within two weeks of purchase.

Pearl does a lot of mail order business, and a catalogue appears every December. It sells out fast, so send in your request early.

Continue west on Lispenard Street to Church Street, past the Pearl Paint furniture store, past a futon shop and the rear entrance to The City Dump, a low-end odd lot store. On the corner of Church Street, turn left and find:

▶ H E M A   C O S M E T I C S
313 CHURCH STREET
(431-5110)

The store has been here a long time, but new management took over a year ago and now all prices are clearly marked, the store is bright and orderly, and the personnel helpful and pleasant. The big drawing cards are the fragrances.

Hema imports directly from Europe, so you could call these gray market perfumes, because they don't come through an American distributor. Gray market electronics, as you know, don't carry the same warranty as the official imports, and that can be a problem, but in the case of perfume it hardly matters. The only danger might be that a bottle is old and has lost some of its potency, but I did not find such a bottle among the dozens I sniffed here. I did find many bottles without packaging, which you may not want to give as gifts, but for your own use, why pay for an expensive package, you will only throw it away. The prices are wonderful: among the super bargains when I visited, there was a quarter-ounce bottle of Ralph Lauren perfume, which retails for $70; without a box, it was $9.50. A one-ounce spray bottle of Arpège Eau de Toilette was an unbelievable $7.50 and a bottle of Joy Eau de Toilette which retails for $82.50 was $41, unboxed. A full ounce of White Linen perfume, unboxed, was $85 here instead of the $150 retail price. Packaged merchandise is claimed to be at least a third, sometimes 50 percent, off retail. When I visited, every lipstick, nail polish, and every makeup pencil by L'Oréal was $0.65, a L'Oréal pressed powder compact was $2.

A small selection of watches by Seiko, Gruen, and Pierre Cardin sold for a claimed discount of 60 percent, and designer sunglasses cost about one-fifth of the very inflated retail price.

The hours are 10–6 M–F, 11–2 Sa. Major credit cards are accepted and refunds given within 10 days. Bring this book, spend a minimum of $10, and get a free gift worth $2 or more.

At the corner of Church and White streets is:

▶ FARM AND GARDEN NURSERY AND STORE
2 AVENUE OF THE AMERICAS
(431-3577)

It's the closest thing to a suburban garden store in Manhattan. The greenhouse sells indoor plants and bulbs; the outdoor lot, every conceivable plant, shrub, and tree that will survive on a Manhattan terrace or rooftop. They also do terrace landscaping and seasonal maintenance like winterizing, pruning, and spring cleanup. Planting boxes of redwood, cedar, or treated plywood come in stock sizes or can be custom-made to your specifications. There are also barrels, hanging baskets, and ceramic containers.

Open seven days a week, 9–5, year round. Major credit cards are accepted and store credit given on certain items, but not on tropical plants.

Continue on Church Street to Duane Street, turn left and find:

▶ S H O E   S T E A L
116 DUANE STREET, AT TRIMBLE PLACE
(964-4017)

Overcuts, cancelled orders, and small lots of women's shoes with
brands like Red Cross, Caressa, Nina, Nickles, Hush Puppies, Cob-
bies, and Bandolino sell for $29–$41, which is claimed to be 30
percent to 50 percent below retail. Not everything is the latest
fashion; you might still find some pointed toes and spike heels
among the current styles, in sizes 5–11, N, M, and W.

*The hours are 8–5:30 M–F, 11–5 Sa, except in July and August,
when the store closes on Saturdays.*

Credit cards are not accepted but personal checks are. There are
no refunds, but store credit is given within seven days of purchase.

Walk west on Duane to West Broadway, turn left for:

▶ E X P L O R E R ' S   C O M P A N Y
115 WEST BROADWAY
(406-9575)

A store for casual men's clothing that is classic rather than trendy.
It is part of a chain that is described in chapter 11: Men's Clothing.
Prices are claimed to be 35 percent to 65 percent below retail.

Major credit cards are accepted and refunds given within ten
days of purchase. *Open seven days a week: 11–7 M–F, 11–6 Sa, 12–
5 Su.*

Continue on West Broadway to Reade Street, turn left and go to:

▶ A N B A R
97 READE STREET
(227-0253)

Under the same management as Shoe Steal, this store sells shoes
by Charles Jourdan, Bally, Evan-Picone, Mario Valentino, and

other top designers for $45–$95, which is claimed to be at least 60 percent below retail. Boots are available in season and sizes are 5–10, N and M. These are manufacturers' overcuts from the current as well as past seasons, so you will find a lot of high styles, unusual colors, and occasionally obsolete fashions, but selection is good and there are plenty of elegant current styles. Many people come here for all their shoes and the clever ones come for the big, twice-yearly sales, which take place both here and at Shoe Steal. They usually start in the middle of December and right after the Fourth of July, and continue until everything is sold and next season's merchandise comes in. Prices continue to come down as selection dwindles; during the last days of the sale, you might pick up really expensive shoes for next to nothing.

Hours and credit terms are the same as at Shoe Steal, above.

Return to Church Street and find:

▶ SHOE GALLERY
162 CHURCH STREET (BETWEEN READE AND
CHAMBERS STREETS)
(964-0737)

There are no designer brands here, and discounts of only 10 percent, but women who need wide shoes like the large selection of styles in sizes 5–11 or 12 from Revelations, Hush Puppies, Life Stride, Enna Jettick, and Dexter. There are frequent sales when these shoes are real bargains, and if you bring a copy of this book, you will get another 10 percent off the marked price.

Continue on Church Street to Chambers Street and turn right, for:

► C H E E S E   O F   A L L   N A T I O N S
153 CHAMBERS STREET
(732-0752)

The only hard thing about shopping here is deciding what to buy, because the selection is immense and the prices—compared to those in supermarkets—almost unbelievable. You can find the very best here, and it will cost a lot less than you'd expect.

Customers come from near and far, and the store also supplies good restaurants and caterers. They do a big mail-order business and can ship for overnight delivery, but not in the summer, when the shipment could spoil. A catalogue will be sent on request.

The best buys are the specials—very ripe cheeses at their most flavorful, but with not much shelf life left. With a little luck you can pick up something wonderful for very little among these specials.

The hours are 8–5:30 M–Sa. All major credit cards are accepted, with a $20 minimum.

Job lot stores are found all over New York, but here there are several within a few blocks. They sell anything and everything that they have been able to pick up in large lots at auctions, distress sales, bankruptcies, and other occasions where things get sold for pennies on the dollar. These merchants then add a reasonable markup and resell their finds at prices that have no relationship at all to the original retail price. The stores are fun to browse in, because one never knows what will turn up. Sometimes it's something very good for very little; at other times there may be nothing that will tempt you. I have rarely walked out of these places without finding something useful.

There are three such stores within a stone's throw of each other, or six, if you count the four separate stores of:

▶ THE WORLD OF DAMAGES
87 CHAMBERS STREET AND 16, 29, AND
31 WARREN STREET
(619-5129)

The name describes the offerings: most are seconds of all kinds, a mixture of semi-junk and worthwhile things, all thrown together. Look your finds over carefully, because what you buy is what you keep. Some of the merchandise is first quality and in perfect condition, but you must find this out for yourself, seconds are not identified. The firm buys damaged and returned merchandise, sells it for bargain prices and, if it does not sell right away, reduces it further, perhaps finally to $0.50. Shoes that retail for $45 usually cost $10 here, but I have also seen good leather shoes for men and women for $6.95. Arrow shirts have been found for $3.95, and there are housewares, electrical appliances, hosiery, and a lot more for similar prices. Not everything is a known brand or good quality, but if you like browsing around for great finds, your persistence may be rewarded.

The hours are 8–6 M–Sa and sometimes but not always 10–5 Su. All sales are final and neither credit cards nor checks are accepted.

Return to Church Street. At the northwest corner of Warren and Church Streets is:

▶ JOB LOT TRADING CO.
140 CHURCH STREET
(962-4142)

The store is also known as The Pushcart, because a lot of the merchandise is displayed on pushcarts, indoors. The owners buy closeouts and odd lots. The minimum discount is 50 percent, but often it is much more. You never know what you will find, but among the assorted merchandise you will always find something useful that you cannot resist at the price. I got an oval fish poacher for $6 when I stopped in to stock up on light bulbs; when I found Lollipop brand cotton panties for $0.50 each, I decided I could live with the fact that they were seconds.

Hardware items, tools, and electrical appliances are bought from regular sources and sold at prices that are among the best in the city. Selection is excellent and includes Sabatier knives. *The hours are: 8–7 M–Sa, 11–5 Su.* Visa, MasterCard, and Discover cards are accepted and refunds given within two weeks.

There are two other Job Lot stores in Manhattan, at 8O NASSAU STREET (619-6868), *where the hours are 7:30–7 M–F, 11–5 Sa* and at 1633 BROADWAY (AT 5OTH STREET) (245-0957), *where they are: 8–7 M–F, 10–6 Sa.* There are also stores in Brooklyn, Staten Island, Flushing, and at several New Jersey locations.

Across the street is:

▶ W E B E R ' S
138 CHURCH STREET
(406-2723)

This is also part of a chain, and every store has a distinct personality. In this one you will find hard goods, housewares, and tools, but I have also seen cosmetics here, and once I bought a wool lace christening dress for $10. Prices are usually below wholesale.

The hours are 7:30–6 M–F, 10–7 Sa, 12–7 Su.

There are several other Weber's stores in Manhattan; the most upscale merchandise can be found at: 45 WEST 45TH STREET (819-9780), *open 8–7 M–Sa.* Other stores are at: 2064 BROADWAY (AT 72ND STREET) (787-1644), *open 9–9 M–F, 10–7 Sa, 12–7 Su* and 475 FIFTH AVENUE (AT 41ST STREET) (251-0613), *open 8–8 M–F, 11–7 Sa and Su.*

All stores accept major credit cards and give refunds within seven days of purchase.

Continue on Church Street to Murray Street, and turn left. You will find:

► GORSART CLOTHES
9 MURRAY STREET
(962-0024)

Take the elevator—to the right of the walk-up entrance—up to a large, unpretentious but very neat men's shop. It has been in this neighborhood for sixty-eight years and has a faithful following among executives and officials who like to pay less for the best.

Most of the merchandise carries the private Gorsart label, but it has been made for them by excellent firms: there are 6,000 conservatively styled suits on the floor, from H. Freeman, Arthur Friedberg, Leo Lozzi, and others, in sizes 36 S to 50 XL. There are no Portlies—you have to be trim to shop here. Alterations are free and swift, with thirty-five tailors on the premises. There is Nordica and Lakeland sportswear, Byford and Dori-Dori socks, and Embassy underwear. Shirts by Eagle, Kenneth Gordon, and Siro, in sizes 14½–17½ are priced from $26–$69.50, the latter for Sea Island cotton. Very beautiful, expensive shoes with hand-sewn leather soles from Bally, Salvatore Ferragamo, and Cole-Haan are discounted approximately 20 percent, and a handsome collection of imported sweaters is sold at prices that are claimed to be one-third below retail.

Visa and MasterCard are accepted and refunds given within thirty days.

The hours are: 9–6 M–F, 9–5:30 Sa except in July and August, when the store is closed Saturday.

For an interesting interlude, continue to Broadway. Across the street is City Hall Park and at its north end, about a block away, is City Hall. It's a beautiful building, completed in 1811. Security is tight, but you will be admitted if you tell the detective at the door that you want to visit the Governor's Room on the second floor.

It's a suite of three magnificent rooms, originally intended for the use of the state governor, but now it is a reception suite and museum for portraits, sculpture, and period furniture. George Washington's desk is here and the flag that was carried at his inauguration. Portraits of Peter Stuyvesant, Henry Hudson, Alexander Hamilton, John Jay, and other early New York dignitaries are by the great painters of their day: John Trumbull, John Vanderling, and Samuel Morse. On the way in and out, you can glimpse a little more of City Hall, like the City Council chamber, next to the elevator on the second floor. *Open 10–3:30 M–F.* Admission free.

Return to Broadway. Walk south, turn right on Vesey Street, continue to West Street.

There you will find:

▶ WORLD FINANCIAL CENTER
VESEY AND WEST STREETS
(945-0505)

and its shops and restaurants, its spectacular, glass-enclosed Winter Garden, its outdoor plaza with yacht basin, waterfall, and riverside dining in season. This is part of the new Battery Park City, a vast commercial, residential, and recreation complex that has been hailed as the best urban development since Rockefeller Center. If you can be distracted from bargain shopping, it's definitely worth a visit.

On West Street turn left, and you will find the street-level entrance to the Winter Garden. A brochure with a map and listing of stores and restaurants is available at several kiosks inside. There is also a brochure with the Arts and Events program, which will be sent to you if you call the number above and request it.

You will find no bargain shopping here, but many shops with a world-class reputation for comparison shopping or the occasional splurge. Barney's, Mark Cross, Bally of Switzerland, Godiva Chocolate, and Il Papiro (with exquisite marbleized paper from Florence) are outstanding, as is the large Rizzoli bookstore, which offers a big selection of foreign magazines. If you are not interested in the shopping here, enjoy the ambience and have a bite or a meal. You can eat at the Winter Garden Cafe near the palm trees or in the nearby Courtyard, where there is a choice of cuisines and price levels. In summer you can eat outdoors at Edward Moran or Pipeline.

When you are refreshed, go back to Vesey Street and walk east, to Broadway, for a different cultural experience:

▶ ST PAUL'S CHAPEL

a very handsome building completed in 1776. Every Monday and Thursday at 12:10 there are free chamber music concerts here, often featuring major artists. On other days you can enter the sanctuary for rest and contemplation or sit on a park bench in the ancient, verdant cemetery, a popular spot with the lunchtime crowd.

Now back to bargain shopping: Walk down Broadway, to Cortlandt Street, and find:

▶ CENTURY 21
22 CORTLANDT STREET
(227-9092)

This is a small department store in the shadow of the World Trade Center. If you have never heard of it, there is a reason—they have never advertised, but their bargains are wonderful and word gets around. People who work in the neighborhood come in several times a week, because the stock changes constantly and they don't want to miss the best bargains.

The store has the most enterprising buyers, who literally travel the globe to snatch up designers' over-production, end-of-season remainders and other goodies of top quality, which are discounted sharply in their two stores.

I saw women's silk print suits with a very *haute* label for under $40, linen skirts for under $25. In the lingerie department a reversible jacquard terry robe by Christian Dior, Barbizon pajamas, and charmeuse teddies sold at very big discounts. Stock up on pantyhose while you are here, as there are lots of styles and colors from the best brands. This is also a good place to look for swimwear.

The men's shop has a big selection of clothing, mostly from Italy —good suits, shirts, and other haberdashery—executive dressing that can be accomplished on an entry-level budget.

There is a cute children's shop, women's designer shoes, health and beauty aids, luggage, and outstanding departments for electrical appliances and household linens.

There are no fitting rooms in the store, but they have a liberal return policy: refunds within two weeks, store credit thereafter, for a reasonable time. *The hours are 7:45–6:30 M–F, 10–6 Sa.*

Another Century 21 store is in Brooklyn at: **86TH STREET BETWEEN 4TH AND 5TH AVENUES (718-748-3266).**

Here the hours are 9–9 M–Sa, 10–6 Su.

▶ **TRI STATE PHOTO**
160 BROADWAY (349-2555) AND
2 CORTLANDT ST (374-1441)

The name can be misleading: this store is an excellent resource for computer hardware and software, video equipment (cameras and players), and everything photographic, from a pocket Instamatic to professional camera and darkroom equipment.

The owner is knowledgeable and quality conscious and he likes to educate his customers and to make sure they are getting the best for their needs. Prices are usually the lowest you can find—up to 50 percent below retail.

The hours are 9–6 M–Th, 9–1 F, 10–4 Su. Major credit cards are accepted and refunds given within fifteen days of purchase.

Now walk uptown on Broadway to Fulton Street, and turn right. At the corner of Nassau Street you will find:

▶ K I D ' S   T O W N
93 NASSAU STREET
(766-1848)

Up a steep flight of stairs are several rooms crammed full of popular clothes for boys and girls, in sizes from Layette to 18. It's part of a chain of cheap children's stores, but they seem to have better things here than in some of their other locations. The discounts are only 10 percent and there is nothing really fabulous here, but they carry Wrangler, Gerber, Carters, Levi, London Fog, Healthtex, and similar brands. Discounts may be better elsewhere, but the selection here is good and the location convenient. Service is minimal.

The hours are 8–6:30 M–F, 11–5 Sa. Major credit cards are accepted, refunds given within seven days, and store credit granted within twenty-one days.

Continue uptown on Nassau Street. A block away, at the corner of Ann Street, is:

▶ 4 7 T H   S T R E E T   P H O T O
116 NASSAU STREET
(608-6934)

A very big discount operation for photographic and electronic goods, electric housewares, radio and TV, telephones, computers, and a great deal more—more fully described in chapter 21.

▶ YOUNG HATS
139 NASSAU STREET
(964-5693)

A store devoted exclusively to headgear for men, but women shop here too.

They carry Stetson, Dobbs, Country Gentleman caps, and Young's private label, in sizes 6⅝–8. Styles include dress hats, caps, Western hats, hats with earflaps, fur hats, berets, and more —the selection is tremendous and they claim that discounts average 35 percent.

The hours are 9–5:30 M–F, 10–2:30 Sa. Major credit cards are accepted and refunds given within thirty days of purchase.

Now return to Fulton Street, turn left, and continue to the next R & R stop:

▶ THE SOUTH STREET SEAPORT
AT FULTON AND WATER STREETS

Eleven blocks of old New York have been restored and transformed into a colorful complex of over 120 shops, restaurants, and galleries. It cannot really be explored during this walking tour; come back for a day some other time and bring the family for visits to tall ships, a harbor cruise, live concerts, street performances by clowns, mimes, and jugglers. On Memorial Day, Independence Day, Labor Day, and New Year's Eve there are spectacular, musically choreographed fireworks that can be viewed from a table in one of the river-view restaurants. Today, just rest your feet and enjoy the festive atmosphere. You can pick up brochures and maps to plan your next visit at the offices of the Seaport Marketplace, 19 Fulton Street, 2 Floor, next door to Gianni's restaurant.

In warm weather, you can have a snack outdoors at Gianni's or at the Cafe Fledermaus across the street, and watch the free entertainment: jugglers, unicyclists, mimes, and acrobats perform in the middle of the pedestrian mall.

The Seaport is a major tourist attraction and shops are arranged for browsing, which can be fascinating. Abercrombie & Fitch used to have a big store on Madison Avenue, where they outfitted polo teams and Arctic expeditions. Here they sell good, classic clothes for men and women and all sorts of equipment for exercise and active sports. In the Seaport there also are shops devoted entirely to sea shells, preserved butterfly wings, music boxes, adult games, nautical toys for children, and imports from Ireland. The New York Fan Club sells clothes with logos of local sports teams and United Stars of America has all sorts of clothing for kids and adults, decorated with cartoon characters. J. Crew, the sportswear company who sold only through their own catalogue until now, opened their first retail store here. Brookstone, another famous catalogue house for all sorts of gadgets, now lets you try before you buy in their Seaport retail shop. There are two bookshops and numerous other clothing stores. The prices are strictly retail. For bargains you have to wait for the sales.

The seaport has a telephone hotline: (212) SEA-PORT, for information about events, stores, and restaurants.

Now back to bargain shopping. Return to Water Street, turn left, and continue to:

▶ E S S E N T I A L   P R O D U C T S
90 WATER STREET (NEAR WALL STREET)
(344-4288)

This is the best source in town for perfume reproductions. The company's main business is making flavoring extracts for the food industry; the Naudet perfumes, which they make and sell, were originally a hobby for the owner, but over the years this has grown into an important part of their business because the quality is excellent.

The store, established in 1895, looks like an old-fashioned apothecary with big glass-stoppered bottles for you to sniff. The fragrances are fairly faithful "interpretations" of 48 popular perfumes and 18 men's colognes. Here they cost only $19 per ounce, $11 per half ounce for the perfumes, $10 for four ounces of men's cologne. They are packaged in simple glass bottles, nicely boxed. Free gift wrapping is available. If you want your scent in a spray bottle, Naudet carries the Giraffe brand—crystal bottles with reliable atomizer sprays, for $7.50–$25. For a sumptuous gift you can give a full ounce of perfume and an elegant spray bottle and spend no more than $44.

How can they do it at these prices? It does not really cost very much to make the ounce of liquid in a good bottle of perfume. The money goes for extravagant packaging and advertising, import duties, expensive overhead, and retail markup. Here you buy directly from the producer, who has a low overhead, never advertises, and does not spend a fortune on packaging. You are only paying for what you really want—the fragrance.

Mail order customers receive a price list and several scented sample cards. Although the interpretations are close to the originals, it is possible that they will smell quite different on your skin. That could happen with any perfume, at any price. You smell something lovely on a friend, you buy it, and then discover that on you the scent is different. Not to worry—a disappointing bottle from here can be returned for exchange or a full refund within thirty days.

The hours are: 9–6 M–F. Credit cards are not accepted, but personal checks are.

Now you may be ready to collapse, so go around the corner to Harry's bar at Hanover Square and rub shoulders with the Wall Street crowd. Or go back to the Seaport for a leisurely dinner in a restaurant with river view. There is a taxi stand at the corner of Water and Fulton streets. The #15 bus goes along Water Street, through parts of Chinatown and the Lower East Side and then up First Avenue. You can wait for it on a park bench across the street from the taxi stand. Catch the 4, 5, J, Z, or M subway trains at Broadway and Fulton Street and the 2 or 3 lines at Fulton and William streets.

Orchard Street Walking Tour · · · Orchard Street Walking Tour · · · Orchard Street Walking Tour

HOUSTON

PRINCE

SPRING

KENMARE

BROOME

GRAND

HOWARD

CANAL

BAYARD

CANAL

PELL
DOYERS

CHATHAM SQUARE

BROADWAY

CROSBY

LAFAYETTE

CENTRE

BAXTER

MULBERRY

MOTT

ELIZABETH

HESTER

BOWERY

B O W E R Y

CHRYSTIE

FORSYTH

DELANCEY

FORSYTH

ELDRIDGE

ALLEN

STANTON

RIVINGTON

ORCHARD

LUDLOW

ESSEX

ESSEX

HESTER

GRAND

BROOME

ALLEN

HESTER

CANAL

MANHATTAN BRIDGE

DIVISION DIVISION

Orchard Street Walking Tour · · · Orchard Street Walking Tour · · · Orchard Street Walking Tour · · · Orchard Street Walking Tour

NO SWEATSHOPS, TOP FASHIONS

ORCHARD STREET WALKING TOUR

In the early nineteenth century this was the best shopping area in New York, with pushcart vendors as well as elegant shops and New York's first department stores. At the turn of this century East European immigrants came here straight from Ellis Island, lived in tenements, worked in sweatshops, eventually prospered, and moved away. Not much is left of this teeming, colorful community now, except a few shopping streets. Businesses that started on pushcarts grew into small stores, however, and some have endured, run by descendants of the pushcart pioneers. The stores may not have changed much since the early days, but the merchandise they sell has changed a lot. No longer do they cater to the poor people of the surrounding neighborhood, but to prosperous, sophisticated shoppers who live elsewhere and come here for upscale bargains, because one thing has not changed: prices here will be at least 20 percent below retail, often even lower.

Service can also be better than that in department stores since you will often be dealing with the owners; in fact, the general absence of chain stores contributes to the neighborhood's atmosphere; you may feel that you have stepped into a time capsule that shows you how things used to be.

Some modern customs are observed: most stores accept credit

cards and will ship purchases via UPS, but many will give store credit only, no refunds. Ask before you buy.

Business hours tend to be erratic, with stores sometimes opening late and closing at 5:00 P.M. or earlier, even when the posted hours are longer. The area is perfectly safe during daylight hours, but most of the people who work there leave before dark, and so should you.

Most merchants observe the Jewish Sabbath—they close early on Friday and remain closed Saturday and on all Jewish holy days. Sunday is the busiest day of the week, when upper Orchard Street becomes a pedestrian mall, where large crowds stroll and shop. Let's join them.

Come down on the Second Avenue bus, and get off at the corner of Houston and Forsyth streets, or take the F train to the Broadway-Lafayette station. Walk east on Houston Street and you are on Gourmet Row—Lower East Side version.

▶ YONAH SCHIMMEL
137 EAST HOUSTON STREET
(477-2858)

Freshly baked corn muffins are served every morning, made from corn ground right on the premises. They are quickly snapped up by breakfast regulars, so come early if you want a taste. Schimmel's main claim to fame is handmade knishes: thin, crusty pockets of dough, filled with potato, kasha, cheese, or spinach. On the walls are photographs of the rich and powerful of several generations, all eating knishes—a ritual as obligatory as kissing babies in New York political circles. One knish makes a nice cheap lunch, perhaps with a cup of borscht or a glass of homemade yogurt. For a sweet (but not too sweet) treat, there is apple strudel, and the coffee is good. Everything can be eaten here or taken out, and everything is reasonable.

For entertaining, take home some of their miniature knishes, franks in blankets, or tiny egg rolls. These make good finger food and they are inexpensive.

Open seven days a week, 8–6. Cash only.

Schimmel also has an Upper East Side outpost—for takeout only—1275 LEXINGTON AVENUE (722-4090), *open seven days a week, 8–7.* Cash only.

▶ ECONOMY FOAM AND FUTON
173 EAST HOUSTON STREET
(473-4462)

has a big selection of foam mattresses, cotton futons, and wood futon frames, foam bolsters, cushions, and pillows. They will cut foam to size. They also have replacement cushions for loose-cushion chairs.

▶ M.E. TRIMMINGS
177 EAST HOUSTON STREET
(260-2060)

They carry the kind of braid that is used on Chanel suits, and a vast selection of ribbons, fringe, zippers, and thread. The store is fairly messy, but the prices are great.

Open 9–5 M–F. Only cash is accepted and all sales are final.

▶ RUSS AND DAUGHTERS
179 EAST HOUSTON STREET
(475-4880)

The smoked salmon from the Gaspé, the varieties of herring, the sturgeon and the caviar are unsurpassed in quality, and since overhead is low, the prices are among the best in the city. Still, it's possible to spend a lot of money here and you may not feel these prices are low, until you have compared them with those in a more expensive neighborhood.

Russ also carries the best in imported olive oil, vinegar, coffee, mustard, jam, dried fruit, nuts, and hand-dipped chocolates. The late James Beard was a regular customer here.

This store is open seven days a week, 9–6 and until 7 on Friday, except in August, when it is closed Monday and Tuesday. Only cash is accepted, and all sales are final.

▶ MOISHE'S HOMEMADE KOSHER BAKERY
181 EAST HOUSTON STREET
(475-9624)

is next door. Enormous loaves of dark Russian bread and raisin pumpernickel, bagels, and bialys are sold hot from the oven. Prices are often reduced in the afternoon, because the next day this bread will no longer be considered fresh.

Open 7–6 M–Th, 7–2 F.

▶ BEN'S
181 EAST HOUSTON STREET
(254-8290)

is for sweet butter and for fresh pot cheese, flavored farmer's cheese (with raisins, nuts, blueberries, etc.), cream cheese, and baked farmer's cheese, all made daily on the premises. Be forewarned: these products may spoil you forever for the supermarket varieties. Absolutely fresh and made in smaller batches, they really are better. *Open 8:30–5:30 seven days a week.* Cash only.

Continue walking east until you get to Orchard Street, turn right, and you are on the area's main street for fashion shopping.

This is the honkytonk end of Orchard Street, where stores open and close quickly and not everything is worthy of your attention. But among the glitz and the junk there are some fine stores with good reputations, who have been here a long time. Don't overlook:

▶ F R I E D L I C H   I N C .
196 ORCHARD STREET
(254-8899)

Women's designer sportswear, wool coats, and raincoats are discounted 40–60 percent here. On the street level are knits, separates, and coats. You might find a wool gabardine skirt here for
$30, or corduroy slacks on a rack of odds and ends where every-
thing is $10. Don't be deceived by these prices—quality is high.
Coats by Bill Blass, Anne Klein, and Dior are sold at approximately
half price. In the basement, hidden from prying eyes, everything
carries a famous label and you will find fashions by Ralph Lauren,
Calvin Klein, Dior, and similar fashion notables, sharply discounted. *Open 10–5 M–F, 9:30–5:00 Su. Closed on Tuesday.* Major
credit cards are accepted and all sales are final.

▶ K O R D O L   F A B R I C S
194 ORCHARD STREET
(254-8319)

has quality fabrics at pedestrian prices. Their selection of wools for
skirts, slacks, and suits is extraordinary, as are the jacquard blouse
fabrics from Japan. They feel like silk but are really polyester, and
machine washable.

This store is open from 8–5 Su–F. Major credit cards are accepted
and all sales are final.

▶ T I P   T O P
179 ORCHARD STREET
(260-3938)

Here you will find stylish, well-made men's sweaters, which
women can also wear. They are imported from the Orient and
when I looked, prices started at $26 for a turtleneck that looks

quilted, and for lightweight cotton blends. Heavier acrylic numbers were $40–$45, hand-knits and knit and leather combinations went to $69.00.

Open 10–6 seven days a week. Major credit cards are accepted and store credit given within seven days of purchase.

▶ FLEISCHER
186 ORCHARD STREET
(228-6980)

carries women's suits, sportswear, raincoats, and leather jackets with very fine labels. They claim discounts of 30 percent.

The hours are 9:30–5:30 Su–F. Major credit cards are accepted and store credit given within seven days.

▶ FLEISCHER

also has a store for men at 183 ORCHARD STREET (473-1380)

which is quite basic.

▶ SHULIE'S
175 ORCHARD STREET
(473-2480)

Fashions by Tahari are sold here at half price. The store also carries knits and sportswear by other designers and a group of high-fashion belts. Rumor has it that the owner is designer Tahari's sister.

The hours are 9:30–5:30 Su–F. MasterCard and Visa are accepted and store credit given within seven days of purchase.

▶ THE EUROPA COLLECTION
163 ORCHARD STREET
(477-1083)

High-quality leather garments for men and women are sold on the street floor, designer shearling coats and jackets upstairs. There is a wide range of sizes. The owners do their own importing (from Italy and Korea), so there is no such thing as a discount from the suggested retail price, but prices compare very favorably with other retail stores. They also have a small selection of fur hats for men.

This store is open seven days a week from 10–6. Major credit cards are accepted and store credit given within seven days of purchase.

▶ ARIVEL FASHIONS
150 ORCHARD STREET
(673-8992)

Sometimes one can find really nice sportswear here, at other times the fashions are tacky—it depends on what's available to them at the right price. Andrew Marc, PSI, and Import Image are some of the brands carried. Unlike most furs sold in this area, the fur and leather coats at Arivel are of good quality and well priced. They also have high-fashion shearling coats.

Open 9–6 seven days a week. Major credit cards are accepted and store credit given within seven days of purchase.

▶ TOBALDI HUOMO
83 RIVINGTON STREET,
AT THE CORNER OF ORCHARD STREET
(260-4330)

A small, high-fashion men's shop specializing in the best Italy has to offer in both clothing and haberdashery.

The hours are 9–6 Su–Th, 9–3:30 F. Major credit cards are accepted and store credit given within fourteen days of purchase.

▶ **BETTINGER LUGGAGE**
80 RIVINGTON STREET WEST OF ORCHARD STREET
(674-9411)

The store is so crammed full of suitcases, trunks, attaché cases, and other luggage that there is hardly enough room for customers. It's not easy to shop here, but there are good brands at very good discounts. You can also have luggage repaired and there is a collection of old-fashioned and antique luggage which is sometimes rented out and used in period films and TV shows.

The hours are 9:30–6 S–F. Major credit cards are accepted and store credit given indefinitely, as long as the item is unused.

On Rivington Street east of Orchard Street is:

▶ **BERENDT AND SMITH**
94 RIVINGTON STREET
(254-0900)

A cluttered, claustrophobic women's fashion store, with good popular brands like Breckenridge and Judy Bond blouses. Large sizes and half sizes, which are hard to find elsewhere, are carried here.

Open 9:30–5:30 Su–Th, 9:30–2 F. Major credit cards are accepted and refunds given within thirty days of purchase.

▶ **ECONOMY CANDY**
108 RIVINGTON STREET
(254-1531)

is a great source for Swiss chocolates, Twinings tea, Oasis brand coffee, freshly roasted nuts, dried fruit, gourmet oils and vinegars, honey and maple syrup, preserves, mustards, herbs and spices, and all kinds of sweets, including dietetic candy. Prices are among the best in New York. When one importer heard what his chocolate costs here, he found it hard to believe.

They issue a mail-order catalogue and ship coast to coast via UPS.

Open seven days a week 8–6. Major credit cards are accepted on purchases of $25 or more. Store credit given within fourteen days.

Now return to Orchard Street and find:

▶ G I S E L L E   S P O R T S W E A R
143 ORCHARD STREET
(673-1900)

You will climb a lot of stairs in this vertical women's boutique, but the exercise is rewarded with top designer fashions, selected with great taste. During the twice-yearly sales in January and July, everything is reduced to half the retail price; otherwise, expect discounts of 25 percent.

The hours are 9–6 Su–Th, 9–3 F. Major credit cards are accepted and store credit given within seven days of purchase.

▶ S .   S O S I N S K Y   &   S O N
143 ORCHARD STREET
(254-2307)

is a haberdasher where Arrow shirts cost a third of the suggested retail price and $150 velour robes in unisex styles cost $42. Sosinsky also carries shirts with designer labels, sweaters, and men's pajamas at equally astounding prices. These garments are "irregulars," but they have been checked over and repaired if necessary so there are no serious flaws—only small cosmetic ones.

The hours are: 10–5 Su–Th, 10–3:30 F. Credit cards are not accepted. Refunds are given within thirty days of purchase.

▶ T R E V I   S H O E S
141 ORCHARD STREET
(505-0293)

The most interesting things here are the super deluxe children's party shoes, of which there is a wide selection. The store imports directly from Italy and also carries men's and women's shoes, handbags, and men's sportswear. All the shoes are 100 percent leather, except shoes and boots with rubber soles. When I visited, children's shoes were $20–70, women's $30–180, and men's shoes $30–150, except for alligator shoes, which cost $500. The lowest prices represent closeouts, which are usually available.

Open seven days a week, 9–6. Major credit cards are accepted and store credit given within seven days of purchase.

▶ T O B A L D I N I
140 ORCHARD STREET
(477-0507)

Here you will find the best European children's clothes, made of natural fibers with lots of expensive hand detailing—utterly beautiful and quite pricey. The hang tag on each garment has two prices: the suggested retail price and Tobaldini's price, which is generally 20 to 25 percent less. Sizes are newborn to size 10.

The hours are: 9–6 Su–Th, 9–3 F. Major credit cards are accepted and store credit given within seven days of purchase.

▶ S O L E   O F   I T A L Y
119 ORCHARD STREET
(674-2662)

A division of Fein and Klein, this store imports women's shoes directly from Italy. They are high in fashion and moderate in price. Since they come from the same contractors who make shoes for well-known labels like Charles Jourdan, they are also top-quality, 100 percent leather, including the soles. Prices, however, are claimed to be 40 percent below retail. These shoes are made on a European last and therefore come only in B and C widths. The big clearance sales twice a year are not to be missed. Call to find out when the next one takes place.

The hours are 9:30–6 Su–F. Major credit cards are accepted and store credit given within seven days of purchase.

▶ FEIN AND KLEIN HANDBAGS
119 ORCHARD STREET
(674-6720)

This store is large and so is the selection. The sales staff will keep bringing out bags until you find exactly what you want, from a tiny evening bag to a roomy leather tote. There are many designer labels as well as bags by unknown manufacturers that are derivative of them. See, for instance, the evening bags accented by semi-precious stones and inspired by a famous designer whose bags are never discounted. Come here for quality and style at a claimed discount of 30 percent, but if you want a really inexpensive bag, you must look elsewhere.

The hours are 8:45–5:30 Su–F. Credit cards are not accepted, but personal checks are welcome. Store credit is given within fourteen days of purchase.

The second floor of the large Fein and Klein store is occupied by:

▶ LEA'S DESIGNER FASHIONS
119 ORCHARD STREET
(677-2043)

Clothes by Albert Nipon, Louis Feraud, David Hayes, Anne Klein, Umi, and similar brands are sold at claimed discounts of 30 percent to 50 percent. You will also find good leather clothes from Spain, Italy, and France here. Semi-annual sales are held every January and July.

The hours are 8:45–5:30 Su–F. Major credit cards are accepted and store credit given within seven days of purchase.

▶ B R E A K A W A Y
125 ORCHARD STREET
(475-6660)

This store sells women's sportswear, dresses and coats by European and American designers like Perry Ellis, Dior, Harvé Benard, Mondi (they have a boutique in Trump Tower), Jispa, TSI, Nicole Miller, and leather coats by Vakko and Andrew Mako at discounts claimed to be 20 to 30 percent. In the fur salon, prices are claimed to be 30 percent off department store prices, but occasionally these prices are reduced another 50 percent during a sale.

There is a big end-of-season sale every March, when things are claimed to be 50 to 70 percent below list, as well as a pre-season sale in August. Sizes are 2–14 except furs, which also come in Petite and Extra Large.

Open seven days a week, 9–6. Major credit cards and personal checks are accepted and financing is available for the furs. Store credit is given within thirty days of purchase.

▶ B E C K E N S T E I N   M E N' S F A B R I C S ,   I N C .
125 ORCHARD STREET
(475-4525)

supplies many expensive custom tailors uptown with imported fabrics; Neil Boyarski, the manager, is a veritable encyclopedia of fabric information. Ask him how loden is made, or the difference between wool and worsted and you will get a full explanation. Ask him for the address of a tailor to make a skirt or coat and he will give you three.

The store has hundreds of bolts in stock and hundreds of sample books for additional selection.

Across the street is:

▶ BECKENSTEIN FABRICS
130 ORCHARD STREET
(475-4525)

Fashion fabrics are sold on the street level, fabrics for the home are upstairs. Orders are also taken for custom draperies and matching window shades, slipcovers and upholstered headboards, and for other custom work. They do a very good job, and prices are reasonable.

The hours are 9–5:30 Su–F. Major credit cards are accepted. All sales final for dress fabrics and men's wear. For home fabrics, see chapter 18.

You have now reached the corner of Delancey Street, near the approach to the Williamsburg Bridge. If you are hungry, stop at:

▶ RATNER'S
138 DELANCEY
(667-5588)

for traditional kosher dairy food. The portions are enormous and the prices rather high, but the food is good and the place reasonably clean. Free parking is available.

On Delancey Street there are a few chain stores and outlets where things may be cheap, but definitely not quality bargains. However, there are also a few shops on this street which should not be missed.

▶ SCHACHNER'S
95 DELANCEY STREET
(677-0700)

For women, Schachner's has a good selection of robes, lingerie, pantyhose, and leotards. For men, underwear, pajamas, and robes are sold. This is an old-fashioned Lower East Side store, where display means garments hanging from the ceiling and where things are stored in cartons on the floor, but don't let the primitive merchandising distract you from good brands at discount prices. *Open 9–5:30 Su–Th, 9–3 Fri.* Major credit cards are accepted and store credit given within fourteen days of purchase.

▶ CHEZ ABBY
79 DELANCEY STREET
(431-6135)

There really is an Abby who goes to Europe on buying trips and comes back with women's fashions, made to his specifications by small manufacturers in France and Italy. They are beautiful, and bargains for such quality. He also carries chic large sizes.

The hours are: 10–6 M–Th, 10–4 F, 9–6 Su. Visa and MasterCard are accepted and store credit given within fourteen days.

Back on Orchard Street, there is:

▶ LACE UP SHOES
110 ORCHARD STREET
(475-8040)

where women's shoes by Charles Jourdan, Anne Klein, Bruno Magli, Joan & David, Yves Saint Laurent, and others are carried in many colors and styles and sold at discounts that are claimed to be 20 to 30 percent. The Evan Picone Executive Shoe that looks like a pump and feels like a sneaker is also available here. In the basement there are a few racks where odds and ends are on sale at bigger discounts.

For men *and* women there is a big selection of Mefistos, the expensive walking shoes from France, reputed to be the finest in the world. They are not at all handsome, but they are very good to your feet and have a cult following. Alas, they are not discounted here or anywhere else, but they are hard to find and here they are carried in depth.

Twice a year, in January and July, there is a major sale, when discounts can be as much as 60 percent.

The hours are 9:30–5:30 Su–F. Major credit cards are accepted and refunds given within seven days of purchase.

▶ A N T O N Y
106 ORCHARD STREET
(477-0592)

Is this Columbus Avenue or Orchard Street? Handsome men's sportswear and shoes from Italy, rather pricey, are sold here at discounts that are claimed to be 20 to 40 percent.

The hours are 10–6 Su–F. Major credit cards are accepted and store credit given within fourteen days.

▶ K L E I N ' S   O F   M O N T I C E L L O
105 ORCHARD STREET
(966-1453)

used to be a wonderful children's shop. Now it has become a women's shop with sportswear of unknown origin and secretive sales help.

Hours: 10–5 Su–F. Visa and MasterCard are accepted and store credit given within ten days.

▶ UNIVERSAL HOSIERY
100 ORCHARD STREET
(674-1882)

This is what Orchard Street looked like before some of it became gentrified: very basic, with nice people selling men's underwear by Hanes, Muñsingwear, and Fruit of the Loom, men's socks by Yves Saint Laurent, Alexander Julian, and others. 100 percent cotton socks go for $18–21 a dozen, women's pantyhose by Hanes, for $2.25 a pair.

They are open 10–5:30 Su–Th, 10–2:30 F. Cash only. Store credit given within fourteen days.

▶ LARIETTA'S BRIDAL SHOP
99 ORCHARD STREET
(941-9279)

has traditional dresses as well as some for very modern brides who would rather be chic than classic. The white lace numbers look sexy and some of the bare-shouldered gowns for the bridal party would be more at home in a disco than at a church wedding, but as evening dresses they are spectacular.

Information on discounts was not made available—management characterized their prices as moderate.

Hours: 12–5:30 Su–F. The only credit card accepted is American Express, and all sales are final.

Many Americans of Irish, German, Chinese, Italian, and East European Jewish descent have roots in the tenements of the Lower East Side. In the early nineteenth century a group of free blacks also settled here, and waves of immigrants arrived soon thereafter, and continued arriving until the 1920s.

► ## THE LOWER EAST SIDE TENEMENT MUSEUM
97 ORCHARD STREET
(431-0233)

was established in 1984 to preserve and re-create the experience of immigrant life, and a grim life it was. There are photographic exhibits, walking tours, audio-visual presentations, and a children's program that is given on Sunday in the museum's small theater. Plans for the future include scenes of immigrant life, re-created in several tenement apartments above the museum by costumed actors. Stop in or send for a current program.

► ## VICTORY SHIRTS
96 ORCHARD STREET
(677-2020)

Pick your fabric and style, order contrasting collars and cuffs if you like, and have the shirts monogrammed. You will still not pay custom shirt prices here.

Open Su–Th 9–5, 9–4 F. Major credit cards are accepted and refunds given within fourteen days.

They have another store at *485 Madison Avenue (753-1679)*

► ## ACCESSORIES ARCADE
95 ORCHARD STREET
(226-6036)

offers a good selection of handbags and shoes, including well-known designer brands, in a modern store with nice sales help.

The hours are 9–6 Su–Th, 9–3 F. Major credit cards are accepted and store credit is given within thirty days.

▶ FORMAN'S PETITES
94 ORCHARD STREET
(228-2500)

A big selection of designer labels in petite sizes 4–14 is sold at discounts that are claimed to be 20 percent.

The hours are: 9–6 Su–W, 9–8 Th, 9–1 F. Major credit cards are accepted and refunds given within ten days.

▶ SAM'S KNITWEAR
93 ORCHARD STREET
(966-0390)

More old Orchard Street, in a small basement store, but they have several stockrooms elsewhere in the neighborhood, so Sam's stock is bigger than you may think. Anything you find will be a tremendous bargain. There may be silk dresses for $35, acrylic knit two-piece outfits for $10, a whole rack of sweaters for $3, and skirts for $16. Some things are nice, some not, but Sam's should be checked out.

The hours are: 10–5:30 M–Th, 10–2 F, 9–6 Su. Major credit cards are accepted and store credit given within thirty days of purchase.

▶ JA MIL UNIFORMS
92 ORCHARD STREET
(677-8190)

Doctors and nurses will find their whites here, beauticians their smocks, and hostesses their maids' and butlers' uniforms, and they can buy them at 20 percent discount.

The hours are: 10–5 Su–Th, 10–3 F. Credit cards are not accepted and only store credit is given on returns within fourteen days of purchase.

▶ M E N D E L   W E I S S
91 ORCHARD STREET
(925-6815)

sells good brands of lingerie and loungewear in a store that is roomier than most and, unlike many lingerie stores in the area, has dressing rooms, so you can try before you buy. Watch out for cheap seconds that have obviously mended rips.

The store is open from 9–5 Su–Th, 9–2 F. Major credit cards are accepted with a minimum purchase of $30 and refunds given within twenty-one days.

▶ R E G I N E   2
89 ORCHARD STREET
(219-8562)

This is the retail division of a wholesale firm that imports really beautiful knits and sportswear. The buyer used to be a knitwear manufacturer in Italy, so he has excellent connections; he also has excellent taste. Sweaters by Kitty Hawk have complicated jacquard designs, German imports have unusual styling, coats from Diffusion are warm and handsome, satin patchwork coats reverse to fake fur. The selection is good, but discount information was unavailable when I asked for it. Big sales are held in July–August for spring and summer merchandise, January–February for fall and winter.

The hours are 10–6 M–Th, 10–2 F. Major credit cards are accepted and store credit given within fourteen days of purchase.

You are now at the corner of Broome Street.

▶ A&G INFANTS AND CHILDRENS WEAR
261 BROOME STREET
(966-3775)

is a nice children's store that carries popular American brands at 25 percent discount.
Hours are 10:30–5 Su-Th, 10:30–2:30 F.

▶ TIE ORCHARD
87 ORCHARD STREET
(431-1606)

Italian silk ties started at $6.99—or three for $20—the day I looked. There are a great many designs, some nicer than others, but that's a matter of taste. There are also suspenders, belts, and tuxedo sets, consisting of cummerbunds and bow ties, available in black and a number of other colors.
The hours are 10–5:30 Su–Th, 10–3:15 F. Major credit cards are accepted and store credit given within thirty days.

▶ MAJESTIC HOSIERY AND UNDERWEAR
86 ORCHARD STREET
(473-7990)

A very old-fashioned store with mega bargains, run by a sweet, elderly couple. They are primarily wholesalers and everything in the window is priced by the dozen; nylon half-slips with lace trim, for instance, were $30 a dozen when I looked, but the owner was happy to sell one for $3. There were also nightgowns, panties, and Hanes hosiery. They may have other things the day you come by and if they are very busy, they may not want to bother with retail customers, but it's worth checking out.

The hours are 9–5 Su–F. Credit cards are not accepted, but refunds are given within seven days of purchase.

▶ LANNER BROTHERS INC.
84 ORCHARD STREET
(374-0960)

The windows display good brands of underwear and hosiery for men, women, and children, like Hanes Too, Bonnie Doon, Perry Ellis, Chocks, Lollipop, Danskin, and high-fashion hosiery by Givenchy and Evan-Picone. The emphasis is on fashion and on the latest styles. Inside the store, retail customers are not always treated with great courtesy, but the discounts are claimed to be one-third.

Store hours are: 9–5 Su–Th. Visa and MasterCard are accepted and store credit given within thirty days.

▶ LUGGAGE PLUS
83 ORCHARD STREET
(966-9744)

The hours are: 10–6 Su–Th, 10–2 F. Major credit cards are accepted and refunds given within fourteen days of purchase. The main store is at 300 Grand Street. See description in chapter 4: Grand Street Walking Tour.

▶ FORMAN'S DESIGNER APPAREL
82 ORCHARD STREET
(228-2500)

This is the largest of the four Forman stores, devoted to designer dresses, coats, and sportswear in Misses and Junior sizes. Top fashions available at a claimed 20 percent discount.

The hours are 9–6 Su–W, 9–8 Th, 9–1 F. Major credit cards are accepted and refunds given within ten days.

▶ B O N N I E   A N D   T O N I
81 ORCHARD STREET
(941-5868)

The owners of this store search far and wide for interesting hand-made jewelry, whether handsome papier-mâché or heavy gold with semiprecious stones. They work with 180 artists and crafts-men and also have an agent who finds antique pieces for them at estate sales. Most of their offerings are one of a kind. Prices go from as low as $12 to about $1,000, and that is 30 percent to 60 percent below comparable retail. You will find the right thing to wear for a party in Soho as well as for a Wall Street business meeting—all in good taste and all good bargains.

The hours are 8:45–5:30 Su–F. Visa and MasterCard are accepted and store credit given within fourteen days of purchase.

▶ B E R - S E L   H A N D B A G S
79 ORCHARD STREET
(966-5517)

Owned by the people who also own Orchard Bootery and Acces-sories Arcade, this small store has good leather bags by well-known as well as unknown designers, from about $50 up . . . and up, and up, but always at claimed discounts of approximately 30 percent. Anne Klein, Tano of Madrid, Liz Claiborne, and Marinelly are some of the brands you will find here, as well as a good selection of Chanel-inspired quilted leather bags. There are also silk and wool challis scarves by Ted Lapidus and Courrèges.

Watch for their twice-yearly end-of-season sales, when some prices are drastically reduced.

The hours are: 9–6 Su–Th, 9–4 F. Major credit cards are accepted and store credit given within thirty days of purchase.

▶ FASHION PLAZA
77 ORCHARD STREET
(966-3510)

Very nice suits by Christian Dior, Augustus, and Harvé Benard in a neat store.

They are open from 9:30–5:30 M–Th, 9:30–3 F, 9:30–6 Su. Major credit cards are accepted and store credit given within fourteen days of purchase.

▶ FORMAN'S PLUS
78 ORCHARD STREET
(228-2500)

This is a good resource for large women who want to wear the best that's available in their size. Large fashions always cost more than regular sizes and they seem expensive here, too, but the discount is claimed to be 20 percent. The collection includes good knits and leather clothing, as well as sportswear, dresses, and a few coats. Forget The Forgotten Woman and her retail prices—look here first.

The hours are 9–6 Su–W, 9–8 Th, 9–1 F. They accept major credit cards and give refunds within ten days.

▶ FORMAN'S COAT ANNEX
78 ORCHARD STREET
(228-2500)

A separate store for coats was recently added to the other Forman stores. *The hours are 9–6 Su–W, 9–8 Th, 9–1 F.* Here, too, major credit cards are accepted and refunds given within ten days.

▶ E I S N E R   B R O T H E R S
76 ORCHARD STREET
(475-6868)

This is a store for sweatshirts and T-shirts, in sizes from Infant to Extra Large and in a vast selection of colors. It is really a wholesale house, but consumers can buy single samples.

The hours are 8:30–6 Su–Th, 8:30–12:30 F. Credit cards are not accepted, and on samples all sales are final.

▶ O R C H A R D   B O O T E R Y
75 ORCHARD STREET
(966-0688)

Elegant women's leather shoes by Versani, Peter Kaiser, Evan-Picone, and others, as well as slippers by Jack Levine and Mandolino, are sold at claimed discounts of 25 to 35 percent. There are also handsome leather boots in season. Sizes are 5–11 AA–C.

The store is owned by the people who also own Ber-Sel Handbags and Accessories Arcade.

The hours are 9:30–6 Su–F. Major credit cards and personal checks are accepted and store credit given within fourteen days of purchase.

▶ L O U I S   C H O C K
74 ORCHARD STREET
(473-1929) OR (800-222-0020)

An unassuming little store that has a devoted clientele all over the world, who order their men's, women's and children's underwear, hosiery, pajamas, terry robes, and layettes for 25 percent below retail. Calvin Klein, Berkshire, Duo-fold, Burlington, Vassarette, Hanes, Jockey, Munsingwear, Carter, and similar brands are available. Come to the store, where service is good, or order by phone or mail. $1 will get you the catalogue.

Hours: 9–5 Su–Th, 9–3F. Visa and MasterCard are accepted and store credit given within fourteen days.

▶ A . W . K A U F M A N
73 ORCHARD STREET
(266-1629)

is a shop for trousseau-quality lingerie, lounge wear, and sleep-wear. There are hand-embroidered slips and teddies, some in pure silk, some in the more practical silky polyester, and outfits for super-chic couch potatoes. They carry every designer brand as well as their own exquisite imports, and they really have the best.

In winter there is silk knit ski underwear by Hanro of Switzer-land, which costs less here than it does in Zürich, and lovely robes of cashmere and mohair.

The hours are 10:15–5 Su–Th, 10:15–1 F. Major credit cards are accepted with a $25 minimum, and all sales are final.

▶ E C K S T E I N A N D S O N S
68 ORCHARD STREET
(673-0400)

This is very old Orchard Street, a family dry goods store that has been on this spot, unchanged, for generations. Bedding and towels, jeans and work clothes, sweaters, cute children's clothes, men's down jackets, sweats, lounge wear, and beachwear (in season) are part of the inventory. There are well-known brands as well as some that you have never heard of, but quality is always decent. The styles may or may not appeal to you according to your taste.

The hours are: 9–5 Su–Th, 9–2 F. Credit cards are not accepted.

You are now far from the carnival atmosphere of upper Orchard Street. Here the stores are well-established, and faithful customers come more to shop than to browse.

This is menswear territory and includes some very upscale stores. Consider the block as one big men's shop and visit all the "departments". Among the collective offerings will be brands like Hathaway shirts, Acquascutum raincoats, suits by Dior, Hickey-Freeman, Daniel Hechter, and Gianfranco Ferré, cashmere and angora sweaters, and good leather clothes, all at claimed discounts of 15 to 50 percent.

► G & G INTERNATIONAL MEN'S FASHIONS
62 ORCHARD STREET
(431-4530)

► PENN GARDEN HABERDASHERY
58 ORCHARD STREET
(431-8464)

Hours at both stores are 9–6 Su–W, 9–8 Th, 9–4 F. They accept major credit cards and give refunds on returns within fourteen days.

► EURO MODA
56 ORCHARD STREET
(219-3972)

Open from 10–6 Su–F, 10–8 Th. Major credit cards accepted. Store credit within thirty days.

► PAN AM MEN'S CLOTHING
50 ORCHARD STREET
(925-7032)

Their hours are 9–6 Su–W, 9–8 Th, 9–2:30 F. Major credit cards are accepted, refunds given within fourteen days.

▶ FASHION PLAZA 2
57 ORCHARD STREET
(966-3510)

In time-honored Orchard Street tradition, when Fashion Plaza out-grew their store at 77 Orchard Street, they opened a second store in the same area. The emphasis is on upscale career dressing for women.

Open from 9:30–5:30 M–Th, 9:30–3 F, 9:30–6 Su. Major credit cards are accepted and store credit given within fourteen days.

▶ GOLDMAN AND COHEN
55 ORCHARD STREET
(966-0737)

Almost the last lingerie store on this tour. There are always racks with drastically reduced nightgowns and robes here; behind the counter is a battery of bins with half-price bras, last season's models of all the best brands, not a bit shopworn. Ask to see them first. Current merchandise is reduced 20 percent.

The hours are 9–5 Su–Th, 9–3 F. Major credit cards are accepted and refunds given within fourteen days.

▶ SALWEN
45 ORCHARD STREET
(226-1693)

Umbrellas here start at $3, great for people who lose them often. For a little more, there is a good selection of umbrellas by Knirps and Totes, handbags by Stone Mountain and Liz Claiborne, and a lot more at discounts that are claimed to average 30 percent. Knit-lined leather gloves by Fawn start at $22, silk scarves are priced from $15–$35. The Salwen family has owned this store since 1902 and they love to chat about life on the Lower East Side.

The hours are: 8–6 Su, 9–5 M–Th, 9–3 F. Major credit cards are accepted and store credit is given within thirty days of purchase.

Here we are on the corner of Hester Street, approaching the end of our tour. The street is quiet now, but old photographs show it crowded with pushcarts and housewives with shopping baskets. Today there is an outstanding fabric shop in the block to your right:

▶ MENDEL GOLDBERG FABRICS
72 HESTER STREET
(925-9110)

Look for Liberty of London's wonderful prints on wool challis and cotton, Japanese polyesters that really look and feel like silk but are machine washable and drip-dry, incredible Swiss cottons, wool jersey and wool crepe in dozens of colors, and generally the best the international fabric market has to offer. Fabrics like these are hard to find by the yard at any price; here they are sold at bargain prices. Mr. Goldberg also sends swatches on request.

The hours are 9:30–6 Su–Th, 9:30–5 F. Major credit cards are accepted and all sales are final.

Finally, the last block!

▶ E. SIEGEL
28 ORCHARD STREET
(925-0745)

A good shop for women's sportswear, coats, and raincoats, including those in hard-to-find sizes; have you ever heard of size 20 Petite? Siegel has it. These people are coat experts and Mrs. Siegel will find one that fits, no matter what your figure. The Siegels are also very value-conscious and refuse to carry brands they consider overpriced. The brands they do carry are sold at claimed discounts of 20 percent or more.

The hours are 9–4:30 Su–Th. Visa and MasterCard are accepted and refunds given within seven days of purchase.

▶ D & A MERCHANDISE
22 ORCHARD STREET
(925-4766)

The owner calls himself the Underwear King and carries a vast selection for men, women, and children. This store issues a printed price brochure for their mail-order customers and has a big following among visitors from Europe, who stock up on men's socks and women's pantyhose by Burlington, and on items by Danskin, Calvin Klein, Isotoner, Jockey, Duo-fold, Warner, Maidenform, and others. The discounts are claimed to be 25 to 33 percent.

The hours are: 9–5 M–F, 9–4 Su. Visa and MasterCard are accepted and refunds given within 60 days.

▶ MITCHELL'S
19 ORCHARD STREET
(925-6757)

Leather, nothing but leather, for men and women in every size, style, and quality. Some garments are made on the premises, some are made elsewhere specially for Mitchell's (who also wholesale), and some are well-known brands like Sawyer that are discounted here. Prices start around $125, but top quality will cost more. Recently they had a butter-soft women's coat for $425, a men's jacket with a button-out Opossum-fur lining for $375, and a full-length women's coat with a fox collar, lined in rabbit fur, for $1,000. Alterations and repairs are made on the premises.

The hours are: 9–5 Su–Th, 9–3 F. Visa and MasterCard are accepted and store credit given within fourteen days.

Now we are on the corner of Canal Street, at the end of our exploration, but there are more good stores in the area. Some will be described on the Grand Street Walking Tour, some in chapters that deal with single categories, and you will find others if you explore on your own. A little caution is advised—not everything you find is a quality bargain. It's best to avoid street vendors. If it seems too good to be true, it probably is.

To go back uptown, walk one block west to Allen Street and take the M15 bus, which goes up First Avenue. Two blocks north and three blocks west, at Grand and Forsyth Streets, is the Grand Street subway station, where the D train stops. Two blocks east, at Essex and Hester streets, you can get the F train at the East Broadway subway station.

If you are ready for a good meal in Chinatown, you don't have far to go: walk to the very end of Orchard Street, turn right on Division Street, walk four blocks, and you are on Chinese restaurant row. On the way, you will pass:

▶ J. SHERMAN
121 DIVISION STREET
(233-7898)

A very good men's shoe store in very plain surroundings. The brands, however, are among the very best: Bally, Bruno Magli, Clarks, G. H. Bass, Timberland, and Zodiacs, all at claimed discounts of 20 to 50 percent. The store has been on Division Street for seventy-five years and is owned by a third-generation Sherman. Recently a women's department was opened next door at 123 DIVISION STREET.

Both stores are open 9–5 Su–Th, 9–3:30 F. and accept Visa and MasterCard. Refunds are given within seven days of purchase.

In Chinatown, try:

▶ L A N   H O N   K O K
31 DIVISION STREET
(226-9674)

Easy on the budget, this simple place has wonderful seafood, nicely appointed tables, and friendly service. Try the steamed oysters with mushrooms and snow peas. Credit cards are not accepted.

After dinner, walk a block to the end of Division Street and you are on the Bowery, in the heart of Chinatown. Here you can catch the Third Avenue bus uptown or ride in comfort—there are plenty of taxis.

FOR PARKING:

There is a municipal parking garage on Ludlow Street, between Rivington and Delancey streets.

The garage on Allen Street between Grand and Hester streets was a livery stable for many years, before horses and carriages made way for cars.

Ratner's Restaurant offers free parking to patrons in their own lot. Call for directions.

HOUSTON

PRINCE

SPRING

KENMARE

BROOME

GRAND

HOWARD

CANAL

BAYARD

CANAL

CHATHAM SQUARE

BROADWAY

CROSBY

LAFAYETTE

CENTRE

BAXTER

MULBERRY

MOTT

ELIZABETH

BOWERY

PELL

DOYERS

MANHATTAN BRIDGE

DIVISION

BOWERY

CHRYSTIE

FORSYTH

ELDRIDGE

ALLEN

ORCHARD

LUDLOW

ESSEX

STANTON

ALLEN

RIVINGTON

DELANCEY

BROOME

GRAND

HESTER

HESTER

CANAL

DIVISION

A TALE OF THREE COUNTRIES

GRAND STREET WALKING TOUR

About a hundred years ago, this street used to be the home of some very posh shops, including the first Lord & Taylor. Things change constantly in New York, and Grand Street fell on leaner times, but there are indications that this is about to change again. In the meantime, it's a wonderful ethnic mix of Jewish, Chinese, and Italian, and a fascinating shopping street. When you go, remember that in the Jewish segment of this area, east of Chrystie Street, businesses will be closed and shuttered on Friday afternoon and Saturday. All of Grand Street opens early on Sunday, their busiest day.

Start the tour at Grand and Essex streets, or take it in the opposite direction, starting at Broadway (see directions in "Getting There" section at the end of this chapter).

On the southeast corner of Grand and Essex streets is an excellent store for high-fashion fabrics at discount prices:

▶ GRAND SILK HOUSE
357 GRAND STREET
(475-0114)

Here you will find a great selection of silks, Liberty of London and other cottons, woolens, Ultrasuede, and Japanese polyesters that look and feel like silk. Oscar de la Renta and Ralph Lauren dispose of leftover fabrics here at the end of their seasons and the store still has some wonderful fabrics from Molly Parnis, even though she is no longer in business.

The hours are 9–5:30 M–Th, 9–5 Sa. Major credit cards are accepted and store credit given within thirty days of purchase.

Next door is:

▶ KAUFMAN ELECTRONICS
365 GRAND STREET
(475-8313)

The prices are good here and, when Mr. Kaufman is in the mood, he gives expert advice on electronics and housewares.

The hours are 10–5 Su–Th. Credit cards are not accepted, but they will take personal checks from local banks. All sales are final.

▶ KOSSAR'S BIALISTOCKER BAKERY
367 GRAND STREET
(473-4810)

If you like the aroma of freshly baked bread, don't miss this old-fashioned bakery, where bialys and bagels are sold hot from the oven. Bialys are the specialty and they are soft but crisp, yeasty and totally delicious. Take home a bunch for the freezer. The owners keep the brick ovens burning and are open for business seven days a week, 24 hours a day.

Around the corner is a little park with benches, where you can munch your rolls and rest your feet. There is also a small post office that always seems to be empty.

On Essex Street between Grand and Canal streets, Torah scribes, calligraphers who make marriage contracts, and other craftsmen who produce or repair religious articles for the Jewish faith practice their ancient trade among travel agencies, kosher food shops, and some excellent electronics stores (see chapter 21). These are two fascinating blocks for you to explore some other day. Today we stay on Grand Street and continue walking west to:

▶ SHOE REPAIR
353 GRAND STREET

This neighborhood shoe repair shop sometimes has a display table on the sidewalk with an odd assortment of very fine new shoes. Whenever a certain importer has just a few pieces of a style left, Erik, the owner, gets them and sells them for very little—never more than $30 a pair. There is not much selection, and not all sizes are available, but these are good leather shoes and sandals from Italy. I saw Bernardos for $9 and good men's shoes for $29. You never know what he will have when you come by, so check him out when you are in the neighborhood.

The shop is open from 10–6 M–F, cash only. All sales final.

▶ EAST SIDE GIFTS AND TABLEWARE
351 GRAND STREET
(982-7200)

This is one of several stores in the area that specializes in good tableware. Everything you need to set a table simply or elaborately, is sold at discounts that are claimed to be 30 to 50 percent. The famous Jena glass teapot from the Museum of Modern Art, for instance, can be bought here for much less than the retail price. On special order you can buy Limoges, Bernadot, Dalton, Lenox, and Wedgewood china, Reid and Barton, Lunt, Kirk Stieffel, and

Towle silver, Retroneau and Yamasaki stainless steel, and many other brands.

People from all over the country send pictures from catalogues and newspaper ads, and ask for price quotes. The store ships anywhere in the U.S. and has a toll-free telephone number: 1-800-GIFTS11.

The hours are 10–5:30 Su–F. Major credit cards are accepted and store credit given within ten days of purchase.

▶ S U N   R A Y   Y A R N S
349 GRAND STREET
(473-5062)

People who knit, crochet, or embroider will find a good selection of yarns, books, and tools here. Free instruction and assistance is available and the discounts are claimed to be 10 to 25 percent.

The hours are 10–5 Su–Th, 10–3 F. For knitting projects, it is good practice to buy a little more yarn than you think you may need. Most stores will accept returned yarns for a refund, but here you must bring it back within sixty days, so knit quickly.

▶ B A G   2 0 0 0
347 GRAND STREET
(420-0768)

The handbags here have no designer labels, but they are nicely styled leather bags and some are inspired by well-known brands. When I looked, there was a roomy version of the famous quilted bag by Chanel, complete with adjustable chain handle and back pocket, a lot of fashion for under $50. Simple leather bags start at around $30. This is also a good source for small leather goods, especially eelskin wallets.

The hours are: 10–6 Su–F. Credit cards are not accepted, but they will take personal checks and you can get store credit on returns within thirty days of purchase.

▶ GRAND STERLING CO., INC.
345 GRAND STREET
(674-6450)

Really beautiful silver and silver plate, both familiar American pieces and unusual imports, are sold here at low prices. The selection includes anything from baby spoons to enormous punch bowls, trays, tea and coffee sets, wine coolers, a large group of candlesticks and candelabras, and all sorts of Judaica.

The hours are 10–6 Su–Th. Major credit cards are accepted and store credit given within ninety days.

Hungry? Feet hurt? Stop at:

▶ GRAND DAIRY RESTAURANT
341 GRAND STREET
(477-7140)

You can have a cup of coffee, a snack, or a full meal here. Gefilte fish, cheese blintzes, barley mushroom soup, and all the other favorites of Jewish dairy cuisine are at their very best here. The bread is marvelous and so is the sweet butter. The place is a bit shabby but spotlessly clean; the elderly waiters are friendly and helpful. Don't hesitate to use the rest rooms—they are clean, too.

▶ L. B. C. MENSWEAR
337 GRAND STREET
(226-1620)

Good men's clothing at real bargain prices can be found here. Some is first quality, some has small flaws and is labelled "Irregular."

Some styles are last year's, but men's fashions change slowly and everything is up-to-date. Recently there were suits by Pierre Cardin and Groshire in the $200 range, heavy wool overcoats for $225, Pierre Cardin raincoats with button-out wool linings for $145, and handsome warm winter raincoats—black with a fake fur collar and a down lining—for $150. 100 percent wool worsted slacks were $40, and Givenchy irregular tuxedos that retail for $450 in first quality were $130–$160. The store carries an incredible selection of sizes: 36–60, Short, Medium, Long, and Portly for men with bay windows. If you wear one of the hard-to-find sizes, telephone before you come down to be sure it's in stock.

The hours are: 9–6 Su, 10–6 M–Th, 9–2 F. Only cash and personal checks are accepted; refunds are given within seven days.

▶ GRAND APPLIANCE AND GIFTWARE
335 GRAND STREET
(925-8829)

One of several shops in the area that discount electric housewares, this store is larger than most and has a good selection of top brands: Panasonic, Sony, Sanyo, Eureka, Braun, Toshiba, and others. You will find microwave ovens, clocks, telephones, calculators, coffee makers, toasters, vacuum cleaners, electric tea kettles, and a lot more here.

The hours are: 9–5 Su–Th, 9–2 F. MasterCard and Visa are accepted and store credit given for seven days after purchase.

▶ LISMORE HOSIERY
334 GRAND STREET
(674-3440)

This store carries socks, stockings, and pantyhose for men, women, and children, and has a clientele who come regularly from the suburbs for a dozen of their favorite brand. Most of the merchandise is not nationally advertised, but quality is reliable, prices are low, and service is pleasant.

The hours are 9–5 Su–Th, 9–2 F. Cash only. Store credit within thirty days of purchase.

▶ CHARLES WEISS
331 GRAND STREET
(966-1143)

This is another lingerie store that carries Barbizon, Model Coats, and other brands, girdles, bras, and a good selection of beachwear in season. They also carry large sizes. There is a dressing room here, a rare convenience in space-poor Orchard Street lingerie stores. Discounts are claimed to average 25 percent.

Their hours are 10:15–5:15 Su–Th, 10:15–2:30 F. Visa and MasterCard are accepted and refunds given within thirty days of purchase.

▶ RICE AND BRESKIN
325 GRAND STREET
(925-5515)

A really nice store for better brands of children's clothes at good discounts. *The hours are 9–5:30 Su–Th, 9–4:30 F.* Visa, Master-Card, and personal checks are accepted, and store credit is given for returns within seven days.

▶ LESLIE'S BOOTERY
319 GRAND STREET
(431-9196)

Only top-quality shoes for men and women are carried here, but we have been asked not to mention names. Discounts are 20 percent except during the semi-annual sales in January and July, when they are 50 percent. Prices for women's shoes start at $70 and go up to about $200.

The hours are 9:30–6 Su–W, 9:30–7 Th, 9:30–4:30 F. Visa and MasterCard are accepted and store credit given within seven days of purchase.

▶ B E R N A R D   K R I E G E R
316 GRAND STREET
(225-4927)

This is one of the very few places in New York where good leather gloves are sold at a discount. Mr. Krieger imports them directly and the quality is excellent. Unfortunately, he has discontinued silk-lined gloves (which are warmer than they look), but in recent years he had gloves with cashmere linings for men and women, in many basic and fashion colors, for $35–$40.

The store also has a wide selection of knit gloves, scarves, and hats, some in matching sets, as well as knit turtleneck dickeys that can fill in the neckline of shirts or sweaters. Paillette–covered evening berets come in many colors. Wear one to the theater and nobody sitting behind you will ask you to take off your hat.

There is also a fine selection of designer scarves in silk and wool challis, a small group of women's felt hats, and handkerchiefs for men and women.

Discounts are claimed to be a third or more. *The hours are 9–4:45 Su–Th, 9–3 F.* Credit cards are not accepted but personal checks are and all sales are final.

▶ G O L D M A N
315 GRAND STREET
(226-1423)

Another good shop for dinnerware, flatware, and all sorts of gifts at discount prices. Selection is good and what's not in stock may be ordered.

The hours are 10–5:30 Su–Th, 10–1 F. Visa and MasterCard are accepted and store credit given within ten days.

▶ F I S H K I N
314 GRAND STREET AND 318 GRAND STREET
(226-6538)

Two women's fashion stores under the same management. They are famous for a very comprehensive selection of bathing suits and beach outfits in a vast range of sizes and styles, available year-round.

The hours are 10–5 Su–Th, 10–4 F, 9–4:30 Sa. Major credit cards are accepted and store credit is given within ten days.

Cross Allen Street and you can see the character of Grand Street change. Although there are stores with other merchandise, this is the territory for linens, decorative fabrics by the yard, ready–made curtains, comforters, and all sorts of custom work for the home.

Some of the stores that take orders for custom draperies, re-upholstery, headboards, etc., have their own workrooms, but others are middlemen, who send their work to a large upholstery factory, where you can also shop yourself.

Treat the next two blocks as one big home textile store and visit all the "departments." Compare merchandise and prices, but don't compare apples with oranges. You can find everything here, for every budget, but you will find no junk—standards are high. Style is a matter of taste and chances are that one of these stores will cater to yours. I shall describe only a few stores, which I happen to know best, but for serious shopping, visit them all and then buy where you feel most comfortable.

▶ E Z R A   C O H E N
307 GRAND STREET
(925-7800)

This roomy store has been on the same corner for over eighty years and is still owned by the same family—currently the four Cohen brothers. In addition to their retail business, they also supply luxury linens to hotels—the presidential suite at the Waldorf, for instance, has towels by Ezra Cohen.

All major mills and designer patterns are available: J. P. Stevens' Laura Ashley sheets and Cannon's Versailles collection, as well as Wamsutta, Fieldcrest, and Martex. Selection from these mills, including the most elegant and exclusive items, is comprehensive.

The custom department makes draperies, dust ruffles, throw pillows, duvet covers, shower curtains, and quilted comforters to match the sheets. Of course, everything can be monogrammed. Discounts are claimed to be 30 percent, mail and phone orders are welcome and delivery via UPS is available anywhere in the country.

Hours are 9–5 Su–Th, 9–4 F. All major credit cards are accepted. Credit card purchases can be returned for credit but on cash purchases, only a store credit is available.

Across the street is another Cohen, one who has been at this location for only forty years, practically the new kid on the block:

▶ H   &   G   C O H E N
306 GRAND STREET
(226-0818)

The specialty here is comforters, filled with down or Dacron and made from your choice of sheets, which you can buy here or bring in. They will make matching dust ruffles, pillow shams, and shower curtains. They also sell some sheets and towels at a discount. Unfortunately, management here was "too busy" to be interviewed for this book, so we cannot tell you what their claimed discounts are. They take Visa and MasterCard and their return policy should be clearly displayed in the store.

The hours are: 9:15–4:45 Su–Th, 9:15–3:45 F.

▶ M A Y F I E L D
305 GRAND STREET
(226-6627)

Lingerie and lounge wear by Natori, Eve Stillman, and Bill Blass, hosiery by Dior, Hanes, and Burlington, the famous Hanro of Switzerland underwear in cotton and silk knit for both men and women, and all sorts of haberdashery items for men are sold here at claimed discounts of at least 25 percent, sometimes much more.

The hours are 9–6 Su–Th, 9–2 F. Major credit cards are accepted and refunds given within ten days of purchase. Underwear can be returned only in its original packaging.

▶ M & M S H O E C E N T E R
302 GRAND STREET
(966-2702)

A large store with a good selection. For women there are shoes by Bally, Amalfi, Julianelli, Sesto Meucci, Newton Elkin, Rockport walkers, Dressport, Easy Spirit, and other fashion brands. In a separate department upstairs there are shoes for wide feet by Selby, Penaljo, Hill and Dale, Revelations, and Naturalizers. Sizes are 5–11, M–XW. Among the boot offerings are leather boots from Canada that are completely waterproof and salt-proof, in sizes 5–11, medium and wide width, regular or wide calf.

For men there are shoes from good American brands like Johnson and Murphy, Freeman, Alan Edmond, French Shriner, and Rockport as well as clogs and sandals. Sizes are 7–13, M–XW. Discounts are claimed to be 20 to 25 percent and there are annual sales with even better prices. Sales are by invitation, so be sure to get on their mailing list.

The hours are 9:30–5:30 Su–Th, 9–3 F. Major credit cards are accepted and store credit given within fourteen days of purchase.

▶ M. KREINER INFANTS AND CHILDREN
301 GRAND STREET
(925-0239)

Very good brands of children's clothes, both imported and American, are sold at claimed discounts of 20 to 25 percent. Girls' sizes are infant–14, boys' to size 20.

The hours are 9–5 Su–Th, 9–4 F. Credit cards are not accepted, but personal checks are and refunds are given within thirty days of purchase.

▶ LUGGAGE PLUS
300 GRAND STREET
(219-9565) (ALSO AT 83 ORCHARD STREET)

Suitcases by Lark, Samsonite, Lucas, London Fog, and Ventura, as well as designer-name sets in the latest styles, are sold at claimed discounts of 30 to 50 percent in two pleasant, orderly stores. Small leather goods are sold at similar discounts and so are Totes Umbrellas, which will be replaced immediately if they should happen to be defective—this store honors the manufacturer's guarantee. You can also get Mont Blanc fountain pens here at 25 percent below retail.

Anything not in stock can be ordered and the discount will be the same. Credit card phone or mail orders will be shipped to you directly from the factory.

The hours are 10–5:30 Su–Th, 10–2 F. Major credit cards are accepted and refunds given within 14 days of purchase.

▶ I M K A R
294 GRAND STREET
(925-2459)

This is a very basic dry goods store that often has the best prices in town for Model Coats, Barbizon nightgowns, Arrow shirts, Carter baby clothes, and Jockey underwear for men and women. They carry all sizes, including petite and very large ones.

The hours are 10–5:30 Su–Th, 10–1 F. Credit cards are not accepted, but checks are welcome and phone orders can be shipped C.O.D. Refunds are given within two weeks of purchase.

▶ H A R R Y   Z A R I N
292 GRAND STREET
(925-6112)

This is the same firm that has the big warehouse store on Allen Street, described in chapter 18, but here you order from dozens of sample books and have a choice of thousands of styles, including some very handsome ones that are well priced. Discounts are claimed to be a minimum of 25 percent. They ship all over the country via UPS, so you can order by phone or send them a sample or a picture in a magazine, and ask for a price quote.

The hours are 9–5:30 Su–F. Major credit cards are accepted and store credit given within thirty days. On cut yardage, however, all sales are final.

Before you get to Eldridge Street you will also encounter:

RAFAEL 291 GRAND STREET

RUBIN AND GREEN
290 GRAND STREET

RENA CUSTOM DECORATORS
299 GRAND STREET

M & A 297 GRAND STREET

Shop them all, even though they are quite similar.

Around the corner of Eldridge Street you will find:

▶ VAN WYCK DRAPERY
HARDWARE
39 ELDRIDGE STREET
(925-1300)

They have every kind of hardware you might possibly need to make your own draperies, curtains, or fabric shades, at "to the trade" prices.

Hours are 8–5 M–Th, 8–3 F, and 9–4 Su Sept.–June.

Around the corner in the other direction is:

▶ ELDRIDGE JOBBING
86 ELDRIDGE STREET
(226-5136)

Bed and bath items in broken lots are sold here and the prices are often the best in town. If you have a particular pattern in mind, you may not find it, but if you have an open mind and a lean pocketbook you don't have to compromise your good taste here—there are always nice-looking things from good mills.

The hours are 9–5 Su–F. Major credit cards are accepted with a $35 minimum, and store credit is given within thirty days of purchase.

In the next block on Grand Street is another group of bargain textile stores for you to explore.

INTERIORS ROYALE
289 GRAND STREET

MARTIN ALBERT INTERIOR
288 GRAND STREET

NEW LOOK DECORATORS
286 GRAND STREET

FABRICWORLD 283 GRAND STREET

HOMEWORKS 281 GRAND STREET

ELDRIDGE TEXTILES
277 GRAND STREET (925-1523)

HARRIS LEVY
278 GRAND STREET (226-3102)

is perhaps the most upscale of the Grand Street linen shops. Not everything is on display, but they carry a comprehensive collection of sheets, towels, and table linens from American mills, as well as imports like the luxury bed linens from Fabri Recami and Palais Royale. Hand-embroidered and cut-work table linens from China are also available.

Their custom work is a cut above average in taste and color coordination: embellished towels coordinate with sheets and handsome monogramming can be ordered. The usual dust ruffles, shower curtains, duvet covers, and pillow shams are beautifully made. For the kitchen there are chef's aprons in handsome fabrics, coordinated with towels, oven mitts, and place mats.

People who buy their lucky daughters elaborate trousseaus often do it at Harris Levy, where it is claimed that they can save 25 to 50 percent.

The hours are 9–5 M–Th, 9–4 F, 9–4:30 Su. Major credit cards are accepted and store credit given for merchandise that is returned in the original carton if it was not a special order.

▶ SHEILA WALLSTYLES
273 GRAND STREET
(966-1663)

On the street floor you will find a lot of wallpaper sample books, from which you can order at a claimed discount of 15 percent. Upstairs is Sheila's large collection of discontinued patterns, which are sold at a much larger discount. They can be terrific bargains. Recently they have added fabric window shades and re-upholstery to their merchandise mix. There are some fabric bolts in stock, others can be ordered from sample books at claimed discounts of 20 to 30 percent.

Turn right at the corner of Forsyth Street to find:

▶ FORSYTH DECORATORS
100 FORSYTH STREET
(226-3624)

Send your fabric bargains here to be made into window treatments like Roman or balloon shades, curtains or draperies, valances and cornices, bedspreads, dust ruffles, upholstered headboards, lined table covers, pillows, and cushions. They also do a very good job of mounting needlepoint.

Someone will be sent to your home to measure, and then all the work is done in their own workrooms on the premises. This makes it possible to do good work for about half the department-store price. As a matter of fact, I have heard stories about salespeople in a certain very posh department store who suggest that customers buy only the fabric from them and then take it to Forsyth. That way, the salespeople lose only half their commissions—otherwise customers would leave this store without even the fabric, since their custom-work prices are astronomical. Of course, you don't have to pay the full retail price for fabric in a department store, when you can get designer fabrics at big discounts elsewhere.

The hours are 9:30–5 Su–Th. Credit cards are not accepted but personal checks are welcome and, of course, all custom-work purchases are final.

Beyond Chrystie Street the character of Grand Street changes again, and on the next block you will find an extension of Chinatown, where you can get fresh fruit, vegetables, and fish for amazing prices from sidewalk vendors.

Cross the Bowery, which has the best bargains on lamps and lighting; see chapter 17 for a description. On the next block of Grand Street there is:

▶ GRAND BRASS
221 GRAND STREET
(226-2567)

If the finial is missing from your antique lamp, come here for a replacement, perhaps one made of jade or carnelian—they have hundreds. Missing crystals from chandeliers, brass and bronze parts, glass shades and globes of every kind, and a great deal more can be found here in profusion. They also do a good job of lamp mounting. Bring them a vase, figurine, or anything else you want made into a lamp, and they will do it expertly and reasonably.

The hours are: 8–5 M–F. Cash only, all sales final.

On the corner of Elizabeth Street is another Chinatown outpost worth exploring:

► K & F FOOD MARKET
223 GRAND STREET
(941-5564)

is a complex of stores where you will find very fresh fish, fruits and vegetables, boxed groceries, and a big butcher shop. Even if you don't own a wok and never eat Chinese food at home, you will like the quality and the prices of these fresh ingredients.

Good-bye Chinatown, hello Little Italy! Look at the outlandish windows of:

► ROMA FURNITURE
215 GRAND STREET
(925-8200)

The windows may entertain you, but I doubt that the display will put you in an acquisitive mood. The store has other, less nouveau riche Italian furniture, however, which is described in chapter 16.

Now let's get down to serious food appreciation:

► DI PALO'S LATTICINI FRESCI
206 GRAND STREET
(226-1033)

The first thing Mr. Louis di Palo said to me was, "We are family-oriented; we are not a gourmet store." No expensive ready-made hors d'oeuvres here, but a wonderful, old-fashioned store where quality is superb, service very friendly, and prices fit the budget of a big family. The mozzarella, ricotta, and the fresh pasta are made on the premises. The Parmigiano Reggiano is selected on buying trips to Italy for the right amount of ripeness before it is imported. Fresh ravioli and manicotti, stuffed with Di Palo's own cheeses, are always available; for other pasta, call ahead and it will be waiting for you when you come to the store. The prosciutto and the sausages are made locally by small producers and cured naturally, without nitrates or nitrites. Prosciutto di Parma is also available.

The hours are: 8:30–6:30 M–Sa, 8:30–2 Su. Cash only.

▶ FERRARA CAFE AND PASTRY SHOP
195 GRAND STREET
(226-6150)

The ambience is so Italian here, it will give you instant nostalgia. Linger at one of their little marble-topped tables with a cup of cappuccino, a gelato, an Italian soft drink, or one of their sinfully rich pastries. There is a busy takeout counter for everything from cookies to elaborate cakes, and you may see a U.N. embassy limousine waiting outside while the embassy hostess picks up dozens of petit fours for tonight's reception. Compared to similar quality uptown, Ferrara's pastries are a bargain.

Open seven days a week, 8 A.M. to midnight. Cash only.

▶ PIEMONTE RAVIOLI CO.
190 GRAND STREET
(226-0475)

High in the sky, Alitalia passengers eat pasta from Piemonte; on Grand Street, and in another store in Woodside, Queens, pasta of every color and shape is made fresh daily and sold to area restaurants as well as to the public. It is made of top-quality, fresh ingredients without preservatives or artificial color.

Ravioli comes stuffed with meat, cheese, cheese and spinach, pesto, or lobster; tortellini with cheese or spinach, canneloni with meat or cheese and spinach, and manicotti with cheese; all noodle shapes are available in white or green dough. Dough is cut in angel hair, linguini, tagliatelli, fettucini, or partadella widths—from very thin to very wide. There is parmigiano and canned Italian tomatoes. Salami and prosciutto are sold, but not sliced—you must take the whole piece.

The hours are 8–6 T–Sa, 8–2 Su. Cash only.

► ITALIAN FOOD CENTER
186 GRAND STREET
(925-2954)

Nobody here would object to being called a gourmet shop; on weekends the yuppies crowd the aisles to shop for expensive homemade appetizers and all sorts of other specialties that would be even more expensive in an uptown gourmet shop. There are also hams, cheeses, and cold cuts of many varieties, at different price points.

The hours are 8–7, seven days a week. Cash only.

Who would have thought, a few years ago, that anybody rich and famous could want to settle into an apartment at Grand and Centre Streets? Now a number of celebrities live in the Police Building at 211 Centre Street, a magnificent Beaux Arts palace that was once New York Police Headquarters and is now an apartment building in the grand manner—with tall ceilings, large French windows, and spacious rooms. It takes a pioneering spirit and a bundle of cash to live here, but the apartments are unique and within walking distance of downtown offices and courthouses. The existence of this building has inspired construction of other, less lavish, new apartment buildings and loft conversions, a sure sign that the neighborhood is changing. Across nearby Broadway, in Soho, it has changed already.

The Grand Street Walking Tour ends at Broadway. You can explore Soho on your own and you will find many interesting shops, but few bargains. At the corner of Grand and Broadway is:

▶ L'ÉCOLE
462 BROADWAY
(219-3310)

a restaurant that is part of The Culinary Institute, where chefs learn their trade. The food is impeccable, but since it is a training ground, prices are far below what haute cuisine would cost elsewhere. They serve afternoon snacks in addition to lunch and dinner, but the menu changes from time to time, so call before you go.

GETTING THERE:

Get out at the F train station at East Broadway and Essex Street and walk two blocks north to Grand Street, or get out at Delancey and Essex streets and walk two blocks south. The Q, J, M, and KK trains also stop at Delancey and Essex streets, while the D train stops at Grand and Chrystie streets. The N, R, and #6 trains stop on Broadway and Canal Street; you can walk two blocks north from there to Grand Street. The Second Avenue bus goes to Allen and Grand Street and buses #1 and #6 go down Broadway. Or take the 2, 3, or 5 bus down 5th Avenue to 8th Street and Broadway and transfer to a #1 or #6.

The M8 crosstown bus runs across Grand and Broome streets, but not very frequently—you may have to wait a long time. Another little-known bus line, the M14, runs across 14th Street and then down Avenue A and Essex Street, terminating at Essex and Grand streets. The M9 bus originates at Union Square East and 15th Street and also stops at Essex and Grand streets. So as you can see, it really is not hard to get to this walking tour.

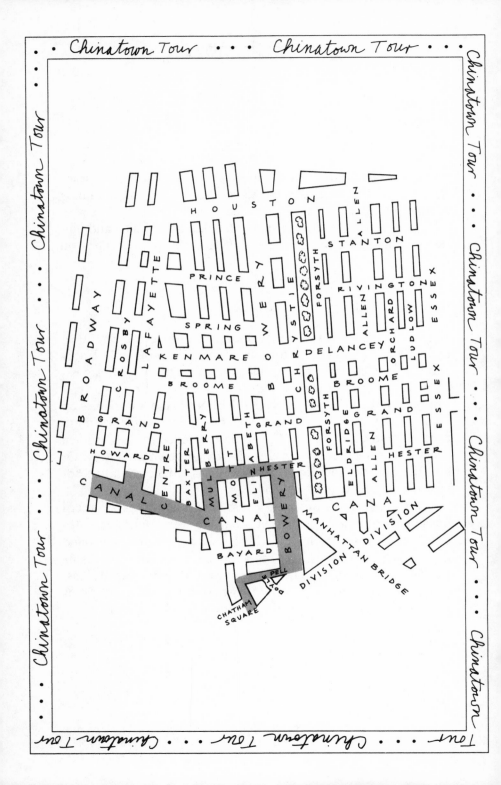

THE SCRUTABLE ORIENT

CHINATOWN WALKING TOUR

There are plenty of tourists sightseeing in Chinatown, and they are welcome, but this area is not primarily a tourist attraction. It's where a large Chinese population lives, eats, shops, practices their own customs, and pretty much ignores the tourists. In many businesses only Chinese is spoken. On weekends thousands of Chinese people from the suburbs and even farther afield come to shop, eat, visit, and feel at home. They are frugal people, so the prices in Chinatown will suit you very well even if you are not Chinese.

Start the tour at Broadway and Canal Street. The #1 and #6 buses and the N, R, and 6 subway lines will take you there. At the northwest corner, upstairs, you will find the:

▶ PEARL RIVER CHINESE PRODUCTS EMPORIUM
277 CANAL STREET
(431-4770)

An emporium it is, with two selling floors of assorted merchandise from China and sometimes from other Communist countries, as well as electronics from Japan. Most of the salespeople speak very little English and most of the customers are Chinese, but you too can get bargains here, although not everything is top quality.

There are some attractive fashions. Short–sleeved T-shirts made of silk knit in vibrant colors were $13.59 when I looked, nice silk jacquard blouses $22.50, reduced from $27.50. Angora and lambswool turtlenecks were $30. The most interesting fashion items were the Chinese-style jackets, reversible from red to cream, turquoise to black, and other colors. They were made of heavy embroidered silk brocade, with handmade frog buttons, padded with raw silk or raw camel-hair fibers, which are warmer and much less bulky than down. They make fabulous evening wraps and were real bargains at $46–$54.

The clothes here carry labels like "Double Dragon Brand" and "Golden Camel Brand" and not all the fashions are interesting, but if you find something you really like, it will probably be a bargain. It's fun to browse and find red quilted cotton shoes with thick black rubber soles for $4.95, a standard feather and down bed pillow for $8.50, cute little ceramic panda pencil sharpeners for $1, and all sorts of other things—some lovely, some tacky.

In China comforters are more often filled with raw silk fibers than with down—it's supposed to be even lighter and warmer. Such a comforter is usually part of a bride's dowry and is expected to last her a lifetime. They are just now being introduced here, and they cost a small fortune uptown. I have seen queen-size comforters here for $165 and beautiful silk-covered ones, in solid colors like Chinese red or turquoise, for about $225. They are feather-light, very warm, handsome, and luxurious.

If you have wanted to take a healthy lunch to work and never quite found the right container, it might be here, among a vast array of housewares. There is also a big selection of stainless-steel cooking pots, clay pots, and of course woks, cleavers, steamers, and chopsticks.

The porcelain department is worth a visit. There are some one-of-a-kind pieces that are really beautiful and definitely collectible.

Each piece is a little different from all the others, so you get your pick. The blue on white teapots for $15, the large bowls for $27.50, and the cachepots for flowerpots in various sizes are worthy of serious gift giving. I liked the "rice pattern" dinnerware—also blue on white—with little transparent dots, which represent grains of rice—or the dramatic chrysanthemum pattern with a black background. Everything is sold from open stock with a big choice for both Western and Chinese table settings. Prices for a large dinner plate started at $5.50 when I looked, and this is porcelain, not pottery.

The food department is where I go for packages of those thin, thin noodles, good for occidental soups and side dishes too. There are also various teas, packaged and canned items.

The store sells electronic equipment, but unless you are fluent in Mandarin, better buy that where you can be understood. *Open 10–7 seven days a week.* Major credit cards are accepted for purchases of over $25. Store credit is given within one week of purchase.

Back at street level on Canal Street there are vendors selling all kinds of counterfeit and cheap merchandise: "Louis Vuitton" bags, "Gucci" watches, "Cartier" watches, all very good-looking; perhaps they will even tell the time, but you can't be sure.

Selling counterfeit merchandise is illegal, but that does not seem to restrict this busy trade. The difference between counterfeit and imitation is the trademark: an almost copy of a Cartier watch may be OK, but if it actually says "Cartier" on the face, it's against the law to sell it, unless it came legitimately from Cartier, and then it will not be sold for $20 on Canal Street. Often the trademark on imitations is hard to read and says something like Carfier or Gurri, which puts it in a gray area, because the intent was probably deception.

Counterfeiting is a dangerous practice and should not be encouraged. Innocent people have died because of counterfeit airplane parts and medicines, which did not perform as expected. The people who merchandise nice watches should be willing to put their own name on them, and many do, even when it's not a famous name.

Not every business in Chinatown is Chinese; there is also:

▶ HEDY'S BETTER DRESSES
274 CANAL STREET
(226-3678)

The store looks as if it belongs on Orchard Street. It has good brands of dresses, suits, coats, and sportswear, at Orchard Street discounts. *The hours are also Orchard Street: 9–5:45 Su–F.* Major credit cards are accepted and store credit is given within seven days.

Walk east on Canal Street and turn left on Lafayette Street. You will find:

▶ ALBERT LAM, CUSTOM TAILOR
127 B LAFAYETTE STREET
(226-2130)

If you have always wanted a suit from a Hong Kong tailor but never made it to Hong Kong, you can have the same service right here. Mr. Lam works for both men and women and his prices are well below the going rate for made-to-order suits. His workmanship is excellent. He will supply fabrics or use yours, but I have not been able to find out if his fabrics are from stock or from sample books, so you really should compare the price of fabric he offers with what you would pay in an upscale bargain store (see chapter 11).

Open seven days a week, by appointment. Major credit cards are accepted.

Across the street is a branch of MARIA, a pastry shop that serves excellent coffee and cakes in a spartan atmosphere. This is a chain with several eat-in and takeout shops in Chinatown, of which the one on Lafayette Street is the biggest.

Return to Canal Street and continue walking east, more for atmosphere than for shopping, except, of course, for the fresh food stores and stalls. The owners are true individualists and entrepreneurs. I have not seen the lady with the eggs for a while, but perhaps I just missed her. She used to come with a big truck, from which she sold very fresh eggs on various street corners. Black tea eggs, which are popular snacks, used to be sold all over Chinatown by street vendors, but one day they all disappeared. The old man who made tea eggs for all the vendors had retired.

Anything that becomes popular in Hong Kong is found in Chinatown within weeks. Right now it is seafood buffets in the restaurants, and delicious soups that are claimed to have medicinal qualities.

▶ E .   N A C K
226 CANAL STREET
(925-5012)

This unassuming little shop sells Seiko and Citizen watches at big, big discounts: you can buy a $250 Seiko here for $105; a good-looking Lorus watch, which is a less-expensive brand made by Seiko, is $28 here; it was seen in department stores for $99. Another Seiko model, seen in a Fifth Avenue jewelry store for $275, can be found here for $40—the very same watch, not a copy.

How can this be? The markup on watches is enormous, much more than the usual 100 percent. The Nacks are primarily wholesalers and for retail customers they simply put a very modest markup on the wholesale price of the watches they sell. Special orders for expensive status watches are also available here, usually at close to a third off. At the other end of the price spectrum are the $20–$30 watches with names like Futura or Oryx. Some are very handsome, derivative of expensive status watches but the "gold," "silver," "black enamel," etc., will wear off in a few months. The movement will keep on going for years, provided you buy new batteries from time to time. The truth is, now that watches are run on batteries, not springs, it costs very little to make them run and the cheapest watch may have essentially the same movement as a much more expensive one. You pay for fashion, the quality of the case and bracelet, for the trademark, and the advertising. If you will wear it only occasionally, a cheap watch will serve well. If your watch gets lost or stolen frequently, it's a good choice. The Oryxes, Futuras, etc., are all made by the same company in Hong Kong, and Nack buys their overproduction. They are good watches, and they cost a lot more from other dealers, in spite of their transitory elegance. New shipments come in every two weeks, and new styles with every shipment. In the summer there are white watches and lots of trendy sport models. If you like a watch in a magazine or newspaper ad, bring in the picture—you may be able to get it here for much less.

Since the Nacks, father and son, are expert European watchmakers, this is also a good place for watch repair. Their Swiss watch batteries cost about a third of the going price.

The hours are 10:30–6, Tu–Su. Credit cards and checks are not accepted. Store credit is given within seven days of purchase, if the watch has not been worn.

The big Chinese supermarket between Mott and Mulberry streets is:

▶ KAM MAN FOOD PRODUCTS
200 CANAL STREET
(571-0330)

where you will find everything for Chinese meals, including fresh meat and smoked ducks, and where other shoppers will explain things if you ask; many of the packages have only Chinese inscriptions, so you will need the help. Don't miss the basement for tea, canned goods, and all sorts of utensils.

The hours are 9–9, seven days a week. Visa and MasterCard accepted on purchases of $50 or more.

At the sidewalk stalls on Canal Street, check out the shrimp, which always cost much less here. They have their heads on, so they look different, but they are supposed to retain flavor better that way. The only thing that costs more here are chicken feet. American butchers throw them away, or give them to customers to use for chicken soup. The Chinese consider them great delicacies!

Before going into the heart of Chinatown, digress by going a block north, to Hester Street. Here you will find another good tailor, transplanted from Hong Kong:

▶ RICHARD YUEN
167 HESTER STREET (BETWEEN MOTT AND ELIZABETH)
(941-9462)

The fabrics Mr. Yuen offers are shown in merchant's books (see chapter 11), so you may get a better deal if you bring your own from one of the sources in chapter 10. He makes both men's and women's suits, slacks, skirts, and coats and will work from a pattern, a picture, or his own sample styles. As elsewhere, you should take nothing for granted, so discuss lining, buttons, zippers, and all other details. Prices are somewhat below those at Lam's, and they may be negotiable.

10–8 seven days a week. No credit cards.

Stay on Hester Street for a block to find:

▶ CHINATOWN FRAME AND ART SHOP
151 HESTER STREET
(219-2828)

They do tasteful framing on anything you bring in, at prices that are claimed to be one-third below those of art shops elsewhere. A nice selection of mouldings and basic mats is available. Round or oval framing, however, cannot be ordered. They also sell the rice paper, inks, and brushes that Chinese artists and calligraphers use.

If the only painting you do is on your face, the bamboo brushes, which are not expensive, are excellent for makeup.

This little shop also sells nice reproductions of Chinese art. They are by no means collector's items, but they are inexpensive and decorative; a framed print can be had for under $30. Signature chops, the seals that Chinese people used to sign documents, are decorative and collectible; a sizeable selection can be found here for $15–$100. If you want four Chinese characters cut in for the "signature" it will cost $25 more. Antique chops, however, can cost several hundred dollars here.

The hours are 10:30–6:30, seven days a week. Credit cards are not accepted, but checks are, and all sales are final.

Turn right on the Bowery, cross Canal Street, turn right again, and go to:

▶ MINH   TAM   JEWELRY   CENTER
170–172 CANAL STREET
where you will find the:
FU   ZHOU   JEWELRY   CORP.
IN BOOTH #15
(404-3015)

When the Chinese think of gold jewelry, they don't mean 14- or even 18-carat, but 24-carat, which is pure gold, not alloyed with anything else. It has an intense gold color and luster and is very soft, but women who wear such jewelry insist that it does not get scratched. Lisa Chan, who owns this booth, has a faithful following of Chinese professional women who like her prices and find her reliable. One should never buy from a jeweler who is not recommended, and Mrs. Chan comes highly recommended. She has bracelets, necklaces, and earrings, cute baby bangles, and cuff links in 24-carat gold, as well as pearl necklaces and earrings.

Return to the Bowery, turn right, and continue to Pell Street. Turn right on Pell Street, and on the corner of Doyers Street, which is really an alley, you will find the:

► G. H. TAILOR CO.
188 DOYERS STREET
(732-0368)

A pair of custom-made slacks of your own material costs $40, a man's suit of your own material, $200. They have the cheapest embroidered silk blouses in Chinatown, but there really is a language barrier here. I could get my interview only because a young bilingual relative of the owners happened to be visiting. However, they do alterations at equally good prices, and for that, sign language may suffice. *Open seven days a week, 10–6 or later.* No credit cards; all sales final.

Continue on Pell Street to the:

► MAY MAY CHINESE GOURMET BAKERY
35 PELL STREET
(267-0733)

I never walk past this store without taking home some curry rolls —flaky dough pockets filled with curried beef—which are just one of many tasty choices. There are all sorts of frozen dumplings to steam, pastries sweet and savory to warm in the oven, and a lot of other Chinese goodies. Their specialty is catering parties in your home or office. Delicious and inexpensive.

Hours: 9–7 M–F, 8–7 Sa, Su. The store closes for vacations twice a year: the first two weeks of August and two weeks in late winter for the Chinese New Year. American Express is accepted on minimum orders of $30.

Now you come to Mott Street, Chinatown's main drag and the street best known to tourists. At the corner is the:

▶ ORIENTAL DRESS CO.
38 MOTT STREET
(349-0818)

where Chinese women order their traditional dresses. They may not wear them often, but for certain occasions, like weddings, they are de rigueur. This place has a fine reputation, and is *open 7 days a week, 10–5.* Credit cards are not accepted and all sales are final.

Turn north (right) a few yards to find:

▶ NEW CATHAY HARDWARE
49 MOTT STREET
(962-6648)

This is a good source for the woks, steamers, cleavers, electric rice cookers, and other utensils you will need to cook Chinese food at home. The grocery carts, baking and steaming racks, and other non-Chinese items are also well priced. *Open 7 days a week, 10–8:30.* Visa and MasterCard are accepted and store credit given within fourteen days.

Turn south on Mott (the opposite direction) and head toward:

▶ BEIJING ARTS AND CRAFTS
34A MOTT STREET
(732-3181)

The owner travels to China several times a year to buy the hand-made things he sells in his little boutique. They are different every time I look, but there is always something lovely for sale here. I particularly liked the cloisonné birds and other animals made of enamel on silver or copper—the silver birds are outstanding, shimmering in many shades of blue and priced in the neighborhood of $80. There is cloisonné, jade, and ivory jewelry, and loose beads if you string your own necklaces.

Open 7 days a week, 10–7:30. American Express and Discover cards or personal checks are accepted. All sales are final.

▶ WING ON WO AND CO.
26 MOTT STREET
(962-3577)

This is the place for Chinese dinnerware and other porcelain, available in great selection. I admired some elegant dishes with a soft celadon glaze and no other decoration, but it was just one of many patterns available here. Everything is sold from open stock, and you can assemble both Oriental- and Western-style table settings. There is also a big selection of serving bowls and platters, teapots with bamboo or porcelain handles, mugs with optional lids, and Western-style teacups and saucers, including a handsome plain white one for $3.50 a set.

Other porcelain items include a collection of ginger jars that would make elegant lamp bases for $35–50, and large pieces like really big planters, garden stools, and umbrella stands. Before deciding to buy one of those, however, check the designs and prices at Ewa, next door.

Here the hours are 1–7:30 seven days a week. Major credit cards are accepted and store credit given within seven days.

▶ EWA IMPORT CO.
24 MOTT STREET
(732-0186)

One side of the store is a Chinese pharmacy, where herbs and potions are sold. On the other side and in the back, there is an interesting and well-priced collection of porcelain and other quality craft items. You will find no dinnerware, but a collection of umbrella stands, planters, large and small ginger jars, and large vases. I admired some carved stone horses, antique reproductions about fourteen inches high, which sold for $125. Each is a little different from the others and they would be stunning in pairs. A collection of modern inlaid boxes would make handsome gifts for $20 and up.

The hours are 10–8 seven days a week. American Express cards are accepted and store credit given within seven days of purchase.

End your tour at another big Chinese supermarket:

▶ K A M   K U O
7 MOTT STREET
(349-3097)

This is very similar to Kam Man on Canal Street, but here the non-food items are one flight up, the food at street level. There is a big variety of noodles. If you like to use tofu as a cheap, low-calorie protein, buy the dried variety here. You can always keep it on hand. When it's been soaked a few minutes, it's great in soups or salads, in a thick non-milk shake, or added to sauces or scrambled eggs. The oolong tea from the Summit Import Co., in gold canisters, is very good and inexpensive.

The hours are: 9–9 seven days a week. American Express is accepted.

You have now reached Chatham Square, where you can catch a #15 bus that goes up First Avenue, or a #101 or #102, which goes up Third Avenue. They both stop at Chatham Square, but at different bus stops, so check the signs.

CATEGORIES

WOMEN'S
FASHIONS

The greatest concentrations of women's discount fashions are found on the walking tours through the garment center and through Orchard Street, but there are other places, perhaps more conveniently located, where one can do very well indeed. Location is important, because in most fashion outlets the stock changes constantly and one needs to visit often to find the best bargains.

▶ DAMAGES
768 MADISON AVENUE (BETWEEN 64TH AND 65TH STREETS)
(535-9030)

The name is misleading—a leftover from previous management; there are no damaged goods here now. What this store carries are women's first-quality high fashions from Italy, which they buy as job lots, overruns, and distress merchandise from other retailers. They are very good at this and therefore can offer fashions by Armani, Versace, Ungaro, Burani, and similar designers at rock-bottom prices. They sell whatever they can get on their terms, so the stock changes constantly, and you may have to be lucky to find exactly what you need. But when you do, you may find a garment that originally retailed at $500 for $100. Discounts like this are the rule here, not the exception.

Don't miss their end-of-season sale in August, when every garment, regardless of its original retail price, is $50.

Sizes usually are 6–16, but sometimes smaller or larger sizes are available; if that's what you need, call before you come in. *The hours are 10–6 M–Sa* and major credit cards are accepted. Exchanges are possible, refunds are not, and they don't ship—you carry your bargains.

▶ SCALERA OUTLET
790 MADISON AVENUE, SUITE 301
(517-7417)

The street-level Scalera store at 794 Madison Avenue sells exquisite Italian knits. The store is small, and when just a few pieces of a style are left, they go to the outlet to be sold at 30 to 60 percent less. What you will find depends on the season: there is cashmere in January, cotton in August, and a lot of good 100 percent wool the rest of the year. If you like quality knits, you should look here often.

The hours are: 10–5 M–F. Major credit cards are accepted, and all sales are final.

▶ TERRY GRAF
16 WEST 55TH STREET
(206-4014)

This is an off-street shop that closes out top couture fashions at prices that are claimed to be 75 to 85 percent below suggested retail. The biggest names and the most exclusive collections are represented, but everything is one of a kind and nothing can be re-ordered. The stock changes all the time and there are usually about 450 garments on hand. About 60 percent are current styles, the others classics from previous seasons. You might find a Valentino cape, a Bill Blass dress, or a real Chanel suit for hundreds of dollars instead of thousands. Prices start around a hundred dollars, and although most things cost more, they are still incredible bargains.

Shopping is by appointment, between the hours of 9–6 M–F, 9–8 Th, and 9–2 Sa. When you call the above number, you will get an answering service, and during business hours someone will return the call within the hour, to make an appointment. Major credit cards and personal checks are accepted and refunds given within seven days of purchase.

Only for tailored suits:

▶ S A I N T   L A U R I E
897 BROADWAY, AT 20TH STREET
(473-0100)

In addition to the men's clothes described in chapter 11, this firm makes man-tailored suits for women. Career uniforms—suits that look as much like a man's suit as possible—are going out of fashion, so now there are also more feminine styles, hand-tailored and made of superb fabrics. They come in a variety of jacket and skirt styles. Prices range from $400–$600, which is claimed to be 30 percent below retail. That's a bit of cash, but these suits are classic in style and very well made, so they really are wardrobe investments.

Unlike women's suits elsewhere, the sizes here are 4–16 Short, Medium, and Long, to insure good fit. Alterations are free, and the management recommends that you take your suit to the alteration department, even if it seems to fit perfectly. Let the experts check the fit—they may be more critical than you are. There are semi-annual sales and a warehouse sale, usually in February, when whatever is left sells for very little. Call the store for dates.

The hours are 9:30–6 M, T, W, Sa, 9:30–7:30 Th, 12–5 Su. Closed Sundays in July and August and closed for vacation the last week of July and the first week of August.

▶ TOM KLEINER'S PERSONAL COLLECTION
166 FIFTH AVENUE
(924-3444)

When the present head of Saint Laurie was a little boy, Tom Kleiner worked for his grandfather and he learned the business well. Now he specializes in tailored fashions for women, designed by him and made for him of very good fabrics. He carries bright colors and pastels in feminine styles as well as the strictly man-tailored suits.

There are also silk blouses that match or coordinate with the suits, and dyed-to-match knit tops.

All skirts and jackets are sold separately, so even if you are a different size above and below the waist, you can assemble a perfectly fitting suit.

The hours are 10–6, M–Sa, 10–8 Th, 11–5 Su. Major credit cards are accepted.

▶ DAFFY'S
III FIFTH AVENUE (18TH STREET)
(529-4477)
335 MADISON AVENUE, AT 44TH STREET
(557-4422)

When Daffy's, a well-known Paramus, N.J., fashion discount store, established a foothold in Manhattan, the first impression was disappointing: "Nobody here," we complained, "wears clothes like these," but a second look, a year later, revised the impression. What you find now are very wearable, fashionable clothes at terrific discounts. Often the labels have been removed and the styles may or may not be current, but there are many classics and discounts are claimed to be at least 50 percent, 70 to 80 percent on last season's styles.

You will find dresses, coats, and suits, accessories, lingerie, active wear, shoes (some with the Perry Ellis label), hats, hosiery, accessories, leather goods, and gifts. The jewelry department sells both fine and better costume jewelry, and had an impressive collection of silver pieces the day I looked. No ivory, leather from endangered species, or fur is sold at Daffy's as a matter of principle.

The Fifth Avenue store hours are: 10–9 M–Sa, 11–6 Su. Visa and MasterCard are accepted and purchases can be returned within seven days for store credit only. *The Madison Avenue store hours are: 10–4 M–F, 10–6 Sa, 11–5 Su.*

Daffy's men's and children's departments are described in chapters 11 and 14.

In Paramus, Daffy's is on Route 4, half a mile east of the Route 17 overpass. Telephone: (201) 902-0800. This store is closed on Sunday.

▶ F O W A D
2554 BROADWAY (AT 96TH STREET)
(222-5000)

On a rather scruffy corner, the racks of clothing on the sidewalk look scruffy too, but stop and look at them more closely. You will find some very nice clothes, with designer labels intact. Enter the store and discover two floors of men's and women's clothes of similar quality. What's extraordinary here are the prices: for women they start in the teens and don't go much over $60 for dresses, sportswear, coats, raincoats, and suits by designers like Oleg Cassini, Dior, Jones New York, Wilroy, and others. You can also find designer lingerie for $6.99 and $8.99.

This is closeout merchandise, perhaps last season's styles, and nothing is predictable: they sell whatever they get at a price, but about 80 percent of the stock has designer labels. Sometimes they get hard-to-find sizes like 2 or 24, and whatever they have would cost a great deal more, even in another discount store. The stock changes constantly, so you find the best bargains by going often, but even an occasional shopper is likely to find something useful at an irresistible price.

They are open 9:30–7:30 M–Sa, 11–5 Su. Major credit cards are accepted, and refunds given within three days of purchase.

EAST SIDE, WEST SIDE, ALL AROUND THE TOWN: *THE DISCOUNT CHAINS*

Check the phone book for locations of stores and then call to verify the address to be sure they have not moved. Hours vary from store to store.

▶ BOLTON'S

has twenty-three stores in New York, twelve of them in Manhattan, from Liberty Street downtown to Eighty-first and Broadway uptown, as well as branches in Cedarhurst, Great Neck, New Rochelle, and Greenwich. Discounts are claimed to be 20 to 30 percent.

The stock changes often, so drop in often at the Bolton's store nearest your home or workplace. You may find a Kaspar suit, a Pringle sweater, or a good leather handbag, and there are always plenty of nice, inexpensive skirts, blouses, sweaters, dresses, and coats. This is also a good source for belts, hats, silk scarves, and gloves.

The hours vary from store to store; some are open 7 days a week. Visa and MasterCard are accepted. Store credit is given within seven days.

▶ LABELS FOR LESS

At last count, there were sixteen Labels for Less stores in Manhattan. This expansion was achieved without advertising, by being very visible, and giving customers what they wanted.

Dresses, sportswear, coats, and suits are mostly medium-priced, very current styles in sizes 4–16. Labels from Liz Claiborne, Jones New York, Adolfo, Harvé Benard, and Calvin Klein (usually the Calvin Klein Sport line) can often be found among the more obscure brands. Discounts are claimed to be 30 to 70 percent and markdowns are continuous—the longer a garment remains on the rack, the lower the price.

The stores are bright and neat, the merchandise is nicely displayed and coordinated. Stock changes constantly, so you will do better if you stop in often.

Major credit cards are accepted and cash refunds given within seven days of purchase. If what you want is not available in your size, you may be able to order it. There is also a layaway plan,

BEYOND MANHATTAN

In addition to all the good bargain sources in Manhattan, a few are worth an off-island trip by subway or bus:

► WALLACH'S WAREHOUSE
3100 FORTY-SEVENTH AVENUE, LONG ISLAND CITY
(718-482-8442)

Quality clothes for men and women are sold here at half price or less. The men's clothing is described in chapter 11: Men's Clothes. For women, they carry conservative suits, blouses, and shirts, as well as some dresses, coats, and raincoats. This is the final outlet for Wallach and Tripler stores. If the stores change their merchandise mix, it will be reflected by the offerings here, so call to find out what's available before you make the trip.

For hours and traveling instructions see chapter 11: Men's Clothing.

► L U P U'S
1494 CONEY ISLAND AVENUE, BROOKLYN
(718-377-3793)

I have been asked not to mention names, but some very good European and American designer fashions in sizes 4–16 are discounted here at a claimed 30 to 50 percent. Sportswear, daytime and evening dresses, suits, and coats arrive early in the season, when top stores in Manhattan show the same fashions at the full retail price.

The store is service-oriented and saleswomen are helpful, but not pushy. They like to give personal service, coordinating and building wardrobes.

Call the store for driving instructions or take the D train to Avenue J and walk one block to Coney Island Avenue.

The hours are 10–6 Su–F. Every April, May, and June, there is a three-month-long sale of fall and winter merchandise, and on these occasions the store is open until 9 on Wednesday.

All sales are final; credit cards are not accepted; personal checks with ID are welcome and purchases can be shipped via UPS.

► A A R O N'S
627 FIFTH AVENUE, BROOKLYN
(718-768-5400)

Take the R train on the BMT subway to the Prospect Avenue station in Brooklyn and walk one block along Seventeenth Street to Fifth Avenue. On the corner you will find a large store full of high-fashion designer dresses, suits, and coats at prices that make the trip well worth your while. There are women who for years have simply gone to Aaron's once a season for all their shopping; perhaps their mothers did, too, because the store has been here a long time. Fashions by Liz Claiborne, Adrienne Vittadini, Carole Little, Escada, Blassport, Gloria Sachs, and others have been seen here and the store carries designer as well as the less expensive bridge collections, in sizes 4–18. Current fashions come here as early as they do in top Manhattan stores.

At the beginning of the season discounts are claimed to be a minimum of 25 percent—often more, especially on higher-priced items. Additional markdowns are taken continuously as the season progresses. Customers are encouraged to call before they come, to find out what's available.

The hours are 9:30–6 M–Sa. Visa, MasterCard, and personal checks are accepted and refunds are given within seven days. Shipping via UPS is available.

▶ U N I T E D   S T A T U S   A P P A R E L
24 ENTERPRISE AVENUE NORTH, SECAUCUS, N.J.
(201-867-4455)

▶ U N I T E D   S T A T U S   A P P A R E L
197 GLEN COVE ROAD, CARLE PLACE, L.I.
(516-741-0860)

These suburban stores are part of a chain that has other stores in Texas and Florida. They use their buying power to find designer-quality coats, suits, dresses, and sportswear that they can retail for a claimed 30 percent discount. There are continuous markdowns thereafter, and eventually a big liquidation sale. During these twice yearly sales you may find something for $20 that originally sold here for $150, or a leather garment for $125 that was $400. Prices start at $9.99, but as you can imagine, it gets pretty crowded on these occasions. Liquidation sales start every year on January 18 and July 4 and continue for exactly one week.

Both stores are open seven days a week. In Secaucus the hours are 10–7 M–Sa, except Th, when it's 10–9. Su 11–7. The Carle Place hours are 10–9 except Su, when they are 11–7. Major credit cards are accepted and refunds given within seven days; store credit thereafter.

► TAHARI
HARMON COVE OUTLET CENTER
SECAUCUS, N.J.
(201-866-5200)

There is a Tahari outlet on Orchard Street (see chapter 3), but this one is bigger and may have different merchandise. I have seen some phenomenal bargains here—perhaps my timing was especially lucky.

The hours are 10–6 M–F, 10–8 Th, 10–6 Sa, 12–4:45 Su. They have another shop at Woodbury Commons in Central Valley, N.Y. *There the hours are 10–6 M–Sa, 11–5 Su.*

► LOEHMANN'S
BROADWAY AND 236TH STREET, RIVERDALE
(543-6420)

This is the address of the flagship store of a nationwide chain. There used to be only one Loehmann's store, in the Bronx. That was during the Depression, when manufacturers were often desperate for cash. In walked Mrs. Loehmann with a large handbag full of greenbacks and the tenacity to out-bargain anybody, and out she walked with fantastic, high-style bargains for her store in the Bronx. Soon there was another store in Brooklyn, and women used to the best flocked to these unfamiliar locations for upscale bargains.

That is how it all started. Today there are 150 Loehmann's stores coast to coast, most of them in shopping malls. Nobody in her right mind would traipse around the garment district with a satchel stuffed with cash. All Loehmann's stores are in better neighborhoods than the original two, but none are in Manhattan.

Management did not respond to my many requests for an interview, but it seems reasonable to assume that 150 large stores cannot thrive only on designers' overproduction, samples, discontinued styles and other staples of the original Loehmann's store, because there is a limit to what's available. The bulk of their offerings now must come from other sources, but their enormous buying power and "no frills" operation is reflected in low prices. Price reductions in each store are continuous, so it is possible to find the same item for $90 in one store and for $49 in another nearby, because it has been on the racks longer there.

Real designer goodies with labels intact—both American and imported—can still be found, especially in the Riverdale flagship store. I know a Bronx career woman who dresses spectacularly well on a small budget by haunting Loehmann's every Saturday. Buy carefully, every sale is final, and there are no credits or refunds.

The hours in the Riverdale store are 10–9 M–Sa, 11–6 Su. Visa, MasterCard, and the Discover card are accepted.

MEMBERS OF THE WEDDING

Almost all the bridal fashion wholesale showrooms in America are in one building: 1385 Broadway. On Saturday many of these showrooms are open to the public and hordes of young women with their mothers and girlfriends wander through, braving bad elevator service and lack of personal attention in search of a discount wedding. They don't often get it. The only way to get a good bargain here is to find the sample of a discontinued style (a woman I know found one for $25, and got married in it). If you are a sample size, you might get lucky. Everything else here is usually sold for the full retail price, and for that you deserve to shop in more comfort.

You can have that, and one-on-one service, too, at discount prices:

▶ KLEINFELD
8206 FIFTH AVENUE, AT THE CORNER OF 82ND STREET,
BROOKLYN
(718-833-1100)

At weddings all over the country, the bride and her mother wear dresses from Kleinfeld. This is the shop for bridal and cocktail fashions, where designer dresses for all black-tie occasions can be found at great savings. There is another store two blocks away at **8209 THIRD AVENUE (718-238-1500)** for bridesmaids and modestly priced bridal fashions. During the winter a limousine shuttles customers between the two stores.

At the Fifth Avenue store one shops by appointment. Hedda Kleinfeld wants her customers to get lots of attention and, when they have chosen their gowns, an unhurried fitting. She also suggests that you come in at least six months before the wedding, but when absolutely necessary she can take care of emergency situations in just a few days.

Prices here are well below suggested retail; the more expensive the dress, the greater the discount, so it's quite possible for a wedding party to save several thousand dollars. Special orders and mail orders are welcome: supply a picture or style number of the dress and your bust, waist, and hip measurements and be sure that you have a really good dressmaker lined up for the inevitable alterations.

The nearest subway stop is 86th Street on the BMT R train.

The store hours are: 11–6 W, F, 11–9 Tu, Th, 10–6 Sa. Every sale is final, there are no credits or returns; however, special arrangements can be made at the time of purchase to take certain items home on approval. Major credit cards are accepted.

▶ I DO I DO BRIDAL SALON
1963 86TH STREET, BROOKLYN
(718-946-0011)

You can order any wedding dress here, if you have a picture of it. If you have the style number, you can ask for a price quote on the telephone. You can also get a package deal that includes the dress, veil, shoes, purse, and slip, for one flat price that is less than what these items would cost separately. Prices start at $200, but for a really great dress you should spend about $375. Top price is around $2000. You can order more expensive dresses, but management does not encourage it. A nice evening dress for members of the wedding will cost about $160 here, bridesmaids' or prom dresses will be about the same. Dyed-to-match shoes for adults and flower girls are available right here, which saves running around to shoe stores.

Samples of discontinued styles, which may be a bit shopworn, are sold for half price, brand new current merchandise at 25 to 30 percent discount. There are also beautiful bouquets of silk flowers, coordinated with the wedding color scheme. Six seamstresses take care of the free alterations.

The hours are 11–9 T–F, 10–6 Sa. Visa, MasterCard, and personal checks are accepted. All sales are final and deposits can not be returned after a dress has been ordered from the manufacturer.

SEE ALSO:

Chapter 1: Garment Center Walking Tour, and chapter 3: Orchard Street Walking Tour, for many other listings of women's discount fashions; also Larietta's Bridal Shop on the Orchard Street Walking Tour. Chapter 11: Sym's and Dollar Bill's.

FASHION
ACCESSORIES

GLOVES

Most good leather gloves come from Italy, and if you import them
yourself, you can save a lot of money. This is how it's done. Write
to either of the following:

▶ A D A   C A S T E L L A N I
VIA PRINCIPE AMEDEO, 2C 00185 ROME, ITALY

and request a catalogue. It will be in English and show color
photographs of available styles for men and women. Gloves come
unlined or lined in silk, cashmere, or fur. Quality is excellent.
Prices are quoted in dollars and are about half of what they would
be here at retail.

When you order, enclose a check from your own bank and send
it airmail. A couple of weeks or so later, your gloves will come in
the mail.

▶ ## MADOVA GLOVES
VIA GUICCIARDINI IR, 50125 FLORENCE, ITALY

Their prices start a bit lower and go a bit higher than Castellani, and there are more colors and more styles for men. They also offer unlined, silk-lined, cashmere-lined, and fur-lined gloves.

I liked the leather from Madova better and the cut from Castellani, but the gloves from both are very good. Here, too, you send a check in U.S. funds, but here you wait three to four weeks for airmail delivery and as long for a catalogue.

SEE ALSO:

SALWEN, on the Orchard Street Walking Tour, and **BERNARD KRIEGER**, on the Grand Street Walking Tour

Street vendors all over town sell nice knit gloves of wool and rabbit hair in beautiful colors, and they are inexpensive. Vendors are also good sources for mufflers. My $6 Burberry lookalike has often been taken for the real thing.

HANDBAGS

▶ ## SUAREZ
26 WEST 54TH STREET
(315-5614)

If you like really expensive, big-name designer bags but don't like their price tags, this store is for you. Mr. Suarez goes to Europe and buys directly from the contractors who produce designer-label bags. You can buy the very same bags here without the labels— and sometimes without the signature hardware—for a claimed 35 to 50 percent less. Discounts for domestic bags are claimed to be 25 to 30 percent. There are practical and reasonably priced items like the light, unstructured leather totes, and super-luxury items like lizard, crocodile, and ostrich bags, of which the store has a large and colorful collection. Even discounted, however, these can be pricey.

Mr. Suarez has been in business many years and he has never advertised except by word of mouth, but fashionable women come from as far away as Texas for his upscale bargains.

The hours are 10–6 M–F, 10:30–5:30 Sa. Major credit cards and personal checks are accepted and refunds given within sixty days of purchase.

▶ COACH OUTLET
MAIN STREET, AMAGANSETT, LONG ISLAND
(516-267-3340)

You know the Coach handbags, with their own retail stores on Madison Avenue and in the South Street Seaport. They are made of soft, natural cowhide that's indestructible and ages gracefully; they are also expensive and certainly a status item. The reason you never see them in discount stores is that the firm maintains their own outlets where current, slightly irregular bags are discounted 30 percent, some discontinued styles and colors 50 percent. The outlets sell whatever the factory sends them, which is not necessarily the entire line, but selection is pretty good. The irregularities are often hard to find, but the store does want you to see your bag before you buy it, so they do not accept mail or phone orders.

The hours are 10–5 M–F, 10–6 Sa, 11–4 Su. Major credit cards are accepted and store credit given indefinitely. You can return a bag to any Coach store in the U.S. Other outlets are in Freeport, Maine and Manchester, Vermont.

SEE ALSO:

Chapter 1, Garment Center Walking Tour: Irving Katz, New Star Handbags. Chapter 3, Orchard Street Walking Tour: Fein and

Klein, Ber-Sel, Accessories Arcade, Salwen. Chapter 4, Grand Street Walking Tour: Bag 2000. Chapter 12, Shoes: Handbags at Gucci on Seven.

S C A R V E S

Status scarves can be found in a number of places, but usually not in great selection. When you see a scarf that takes your fancy, for yourself or for a gift, buy it and put it aside. You may not find exactly what you need when you want it. Good sources are: Gucci on Seven, Bernard Krieger, Salwen, Century 21.

FURS

You don't buy a fur every year, so you may not be as knowledgeable about quality as you should be when investing some of your hard-earned cash. When I made this point to a well-known furrier, he sneered and said, "See your broker if you want to invest." I hope many of his customers will do just that. The people from whom you buy a fur should be willing to explain quality to you and to advise you honestly about the advantages and disadvantages of various furs. I think they should also be aware that, for most customers, this is indeed a major expenditure.

On my way through the wholesale fur district I saw elegant customers from all over the world, because the best furs in the world are made in New York. The best skins and the finest workmanship are found here and New York furriers export all over the world. Coats from the Orient cost considerably less due to lower labor costs and some look very nice, but the quality cannot be compared to a fine American coat.

What kind of fur should you consider? Mink is by far the most popular fur nowadays, for good reason. It wears well, it is light, very warm, and it can be very luxurious. The most popular color has been ranch, which is almost black, but Lunaraine, which is brown with a marked stripe, is gaining popularity. Mink comes in many other colors, from pure white through many shades of gray to beige and brown. Female skins are lighter and silkier than male skins, but a great deal depends on how they are worked. There are also small male skins, whose characteristics approach that of the female skins. Mature male skins are heavier, which is a disadvantage, but have the advantage of wearing extremely well. They are often split down the middle, to make narrower stripes. Let-out skins have been cut diagonally into strips and then sewn together again, which results in the long, thin, lightweight stripes on a mink coat. Look at the reverse side of a coat (linings on good ones are always loose) and you should see pale beige leather, with clean, evenly stitched diagonal seaming and absolutely no hair caught in these seams. The let-out skins are joined by means of narrow leather strips. When the furrier wants to cut a few corners, these strips may be a little wider. When you hear people in the trade speak of heavy leathering, that's what they mean. If the back is not pale beige the skins have been dyed, and a dyed color is inferior to natural color, unless it is dyed some high-fashion shade that does not occur naturally.

Raccoon is about half the price of mink and the best raccoon, which comes from Texas, can be light and silky, with a silvery cast. It, too, wears extremely well.

Beaver comes with both natural, unplucked skins and sheared skins, which are lighter and have a velvety texture. Unless the skin is choice and the workmanship expert, it tends to be heavy. Although sheared beaver has an attractive brown to silver shading, it is often seen dyed in fashion colors like green or purple.

Nutria looks similar to beaver, but is lighter. Lightness is considered important in furs—nobody wants to walk around with a heavy coat on her shoulders.

Swakara resembles the old-fashioned Persian lamb, but is much lighter and softer, with a wide choice of natural colors. Then there are the luxurious long-haired furs: fox of all colors, and, for really big spenders, lynx, fisher, and sable.

It is better to get the best quality of a less expensive fur than the cheapest quality of a costly one. If you can't afford really good mink, get really good raccoon. Don't get cheap mink unless you have your heart set on mink no matter what, and even then compare a cheap mink with a really good one and you may reconsider.

Shearling is inside-out lambskin. The fur is on the inside of the garment, the outside is suede, often dyed in high-fashion colors. If you live in New York, choose a dark color for both fur and suede, because city living is inevitably sooty and dry cleaning does not improve shearling. It comes in a wide range of qualities, the finest being tissue thin and feather light.

Unlike dresses, which are always cut in multiples, fur coats are made one at a time, and any wholesale furrier will sell you a single coat. Many will make it to order in your exact size and give you a canvas fitting before working the fur; others who have ready-to-wear inventory will sell you a coat off the rack. This has the advantage of letting you try before you buy. The custom-made coat may fit better and will need no alterations.

For the very best value, buy your coat in the spring, when the season is over and many fur manufacturers have sales. They are not so busy then, your business will help keep the workrooms going, and prices are lower than they are during the busy season. You usually get one year's storage free and your coat will be held for you until the following fall.

I recommend furriers as carefully as I do jewelers. The following are known to me as reliable, honest producers of beautiful furs, where you will get good fashion and excellent value. All are wholesalers who will welcome your business and give you good service. Don't expect to be charged true wholesale prices, unless you buy wholesale quantities, but the prices here will be far below those for similar quality in retail stores. On altered and custom-made coats all sales are final and the customary form of payment is personal check. Some firms accept credit cards if you request it; others don't.

▶ N E U S T A D T E R   F U R S
352 SEVENTH AVENUE
(736-6973)

Four generations of Neustadters have built this business into a
large manufacturer of quality furs. Mink, sable, fisher, lynx, kolin-
sky and Russian squirrel, which is silver gray, are sold here in a
wide range of sizes, from Petite to Extra Large. You will also find
good-quality shearling in dark fashion colors. Hours are by appointment, so call before you go.

▶ A E G E A N   F U R   F A S H I O N   C O R P.
352 SEVENTH AVENUE
(736-4451)

This is the place for very fine shearling in dark fashion colors at
prices that are claimed to be wholesale. You will also find mink
from American breeders in many natural colors.
   The hours are 9–6, but call ahead and make an appointment.

▶ S D R O U G I A S   F U R S
330 SEVENTH AVENUE
(563-1730)

You will find a great selection here: for the small budget there is
sheared muskrat, Swakara, crystal fox and other foxes; good- to
top-quality female mink is for the luxury-minded. The end-of-
season sale starts in January and prices are claimed to be close to
wholesale. Both made-to-order and ready-to-wear coats are available here in great selection. This is also a good place for all sorts of
custom work, like fur-lined raincoats; bring in your old fur for the
lining.

▶ G. MICHAEL HENNESSEY
333 SEVENTH AVENUE
(695-7991)

The skins here are beautiful and the styles elegant. There is usually a big end-of-season sale, when prices are sharply reduced.
Call for sales information and a showroom appointment.

▶ POLIGEORGIS
333 SEVENTH AVENUE
(563-2250)

A manufacturing furrier with customers all over the world, this firm has a large inventory on the premises and can supply you with a ready-made coat as well as a made-to-order one. In addition to fine American mink they have sheared beaver, Swakara, fox, lynx, and sable, as well as some unusual furs: sable paws have the cachet of sable but not the price, and mink paws are sometimes sheared to a velvety texture and dyed in high-fashion hues.
You can drop in from 9–5 M–F or make an appointment for Saturday and you can pay with your American Express card.

▶ WALZER FURS
15 WEST 30TH STREET
(242-6900)

In business for eighty-six years, this wholesale establishment is still owned and run by the original family. Today a father, son, son-in-law, and their wives and daughters run the business, offering a lot of personal service to their customers. Coats of mink and every other fashion fur are manufactured on the premises and there is a large selection to try on. Made-to-order furs are also available. The fabulous Intrefino shearlings are imported from Spain and there are fur-lined cashmere coats and silk raincoats as well. Storage, including pickup and delivery, is free.

The emphasis here is on top quality and fashion, so prices are not cheap, but value is very good indeed.

Hours are by appointment and payment is by check.

▶ M O H L   F U R   C O M P A N Y
345 SEVENTH AVENUE
(736-7676)

Some of the finest department stores in the country, like I. Magnin and Bullocks-Wilshire, carry Mohl furs at sky-high retail prices, but you can buy them at the source at prices that are claimed to be 10 percent above wholesale.

Coats are shown by live models in a showroom with crystal chandeliers, while a member of the Mohl family sits with you and explains everything—at least that's what happened to me when I shopped by appointment. The fashions are often imaginative and created by big-name designers like Scaasi, who is currently designing for Mohl. Prices start in the affordable range and go up from there. In addition to American and Scandinavian mink, there is raccoon, beaver, muskrat, fox, and of course lynx, fisher, and sable. There is also that lightweight, subtle, top-quality shearling from Spain.

Shop by appointment between 9–5:30, and pay by check here.

▶ J I N D O   F U R S
1010 THIRD AVENUE (754-1166)
575 FIFTH AVENUE (867-0710)
41 WEST 57TH STREET (754-1177)

The other sources for fur in this chapter are often family-owned and work mostly in American-raised furs, but this is a giant Asian manufacturer, the biggest in the world, with three stores in Manhattan, eight in the U.S., and a number in Europe.

The garments here have been mass-produced in Asia, with pelts from many sources, including their own mink ranch in Korea.

Generally speaking, quality does not approach the best New York-made minks, but neither do the prices, which start at a very affordable level here. The end-of-season price for one of their mink coat styles was $1295 in 1990. I saw some very nice fur-lined raincoats at bargain prices, as well as some trendy leather and fur jackets. There were handsome fur coats which cost a lot more than $1295, but they were still outstanding bargains and, right next to them, I saw coats that were cheap and looked cheap. Sizes are S, M, and L, so alterations may be required.

When I admired a herringbone-patterned two-tone mink, the saleswoman who showed me around insisted that I try it on, even though she knew I was there to conduct an interview—not to shop. She emphasized that it had just been reduced and was a great bargain. It did not fit me at all, but she declared that it would be perfect if it was shortened a little. What it would have been is a disaster, so, as usual, let the buyer beware.

JEWELRY, *FINE*
AND *COSTUME*

How do you shop for fine jewelry? How do porcupines mate? Very carefully! Let's face it: you are no expert, and even the experts you consult may give you conflicting messages. An appraisal is only an opinion, so be sure you get an informed opinion from a very honest expert. The trouble is, there are people in the jewelry trade who are not very honest with consumers, so you must know with whom you are dealing. Ideally, a dealer should be prepared to give you an education, to explain the finer points of color, cut, and clarity in stones, the different carats in gold, and what each looks like. Some dealers offer a money-back guarantee and let you take your purchase to be appraised, but where do you take it and why can two appraisals be $1,300 apart on a single piece of estate jewelry? This happened to me recently, so the piece is no longer for sale. Had I been the buyer instead of the seller, I would have lost interest even faster.

▶ DIAMONDS BY RENNIE ELLEN
15 WEST 47TH STREET
(869-5525)

This lady was a dancer on Broadway, and between shows she worked as a diamond cutter. When the time came to hang up her dancing shoes, she went into the diamond business herself and she also became a consumer advocate. Some of the other dealers were less than delighted, but her customers feel very comfortable with her.

In her reception area you will find an album with thank-you notes, wedding pictures, and baby pictures from couples who bought their engagement rings from Rennie. Her diamonds are worth exactly what she says they are, and since this is where the diamonds are cut and polished, without middlemen, her prices are the best.

For those who just want something sparkling to wear, of no sentimental or resale value, there are cubic zirconia, man-made diamonds. To the naked eye they look like the finest diamonds. Their weight is different, so a one-carat cubic zirconium (a.k.a. CZ) is not the same size as a one-carat diamond.

They are never very expensive, but they are really *cheap* at:

▶ KANE ENTERPRISES, A DIVISION OF RENNIE ELLEN
15 WEST 47TH STREET
(869-5525)

Being man-made, these stones are always perfect in color and clarity, so quality depends on the cutting and polishing. At Kane, that is excellent, too. Rennie has them set into rings, tennis brace-lets, earrings, etc., by various jewelers in the area.

Both divisions do a good deal of mail-order business. For personal service by Ms. Ellen, call for an appointment.

▶ M Y R O N   T O B A K
23 WEST 47 STREET
(398-8300)

A very busy space in a Forty-seventh Street arcade, this shop sells
chains, clasps, jewelry parts, and supplies to both jewelers and
imaginative consumers. This is the place for earring backs and
other small things that one always loses.

Gold, silver, or gold-filled beads come in all sizes from tiny to
jumbo, and can easily be made into interesting necklaces. They are
strung onto a very thin gold chain to which a clasp is permanently
attached. Made this way, the necklace costs less than half the price
of a comparable one in a retail store and you can make it exactly
as long as you like, you can graduate the beads, and make one or
several strands.

What looks like a ribbon counter, with big cardboard spools,
actually stores an enormous assortment of gold and silver chains,
which the store will cut to any length. They will then sell you a
clasp and send you to their neighbor in the arcade:

▶ F I O R E   A N D   S O N
23 WEST 47 STREET
(221-3320)

who will attach clasps to chains, repair or remodel jewelry, size
rings, or put stones into new settings while you watch, so you
know you are getting your own stone back.

In the same arcade is:

▶ I . R . M .   G E M S   A N D   L A P I D A R Y
23 WEST 47 STREET
(764-6499)

They sell gems to be set into jewelry, as well as necklace-length
strings of semi-precious stones. These start at $6 a string, depend-

ing on size and quality, and don't go much over $75, for a string of large lapis lazuli or tiger's eye beads. There is onyx and turquoise, carnelian, hematite, jade, coral, rose quartz, garnet, malachite, goldstone, amethyst, and if I left something out, they have that, too. Mix these beads with each other, with gold or silver beads, or with pearls, and you can have unique jewelry for just a little money.

The hours are 10–5 M–F. Since this is really a wholesale establishment, credit cards are not accepted.

▶ AMERICAN PEARL
23 WEST 47 STREET
(221-3045)

A presentable, short string of cultured pearls can be had here for $125, a better one with bigger pearls for $200, and up and up. Of course really fine pearls cost a lot more, but these are nice, and they will improve their luster with time. You can buy matched pairs of pearls for earrings here, get the gold mountings across the way at Tobak, attach them with one little drop of Duco cement, and have elegant earrings for very little. You can even get a velvet presentation box at Tobak.

▶ FORTUNOFF
681 FIFTH AVENUE (AT 55TH STREET)
(758-6660)

A large, elegant store at a fashionable address, where jewelry, silverware, watches, and clocks are sold for considerably less than at most other retailers.

Although the house-brand Fortron watches may have the same movement as cheaper watches elsewhere, this is unimportant because even cheap watches keep excellent time nowadays (see E. Nack on the Chinatown walking tour). The watchcases and bracelets here are of excellent quality and this is the best-looking collection of house-brand watches I have seen. For famous brands like Seiko and Citizen, however, you may do better elsewhere.

Shopping for jewelry here is not like shopping wholesale in the jewelry center, where things cost less but not everything on the market is available to you from a reliable wholesaler. The selection here is enormous: beautiful earrings, rings, and bracelets come from good designers and include some very affordable pieces. It's also important that you shop from a reliable source, since there have been a few scandals when other dealers advertised 14-carat gold jewelry that turned out to have a much-lower gold content. Fortunoff is a class act, where you can shop with confidence.

The hours are 10–6 M–Sa, 10–8 Th. Major credit cards are accepted and refunds given within ten days. However, if you are buying a gift, the return policy will be adjusted to ten days after the gift is presented.

COSTUME JEWELRY:

▶ GAEL GRANT
485 MADISON AVENUE (AT 52ND STREET)
(752-3142)

The jewelry worn by those well-dressed soap opera stars often comes from Gael Grant's enormous selection. Mixed with some of your real pieces, nobody will suspect that this costume jewelry is not the real thing. These are not one-of-a-kind pieces; they are similar to what you might find in a good department store, but here the selection is bigger, chosen with great taste, and much more sharply priced. You can also expect services here which are not available elsewhere: the clip-on backs on those large new earrings can be softened, necklaces can be shortened. You can really cheer yourself up with something from Gael, and it's not fattening.

Open 10–6 M–Sa. Major credit cards are accepted and all sales are final.

▶ MANSON ACCESSORIES INC.
1196 BROADWAY AT 29TH STREET
(213-1482)

All that glitters might be brass, but it's very pretty and if you keep the brass polish handy, nobody will know it's not gold. This is a wholesaler, but retail customers are not turned away, and everything is really inexpensive. There are sculptured bracelets and bangles, interesting necklaces that look vaguely tribal, minaudieres, beaded dresses, blouses and other imports from India, well selected and in good taste.

The hours are 8–8 M–F, 8–6 Sa, 12–5 Su. Major credit cards are accepted and store credit given within ten days.

SEE ALSO:

Sheru, on the Garment Center Walking Tour, and Bonnie and Toni on the Orchard Street Walking Tour.

FABRICS AND YARNS

People who know a good little dressmaker, or who have the time and the skill to make some of their own clothes, can have couture creations for very little money. And here, in the fashion capital of America, you can find couture fabrics at polyester prices.

The top dress manufacturers place their fabric orders early, so that they will have yardage on hand to fill orders, but there will often be yardage left when the season is over; a small group of fabric retailers snaps up these bolts and resells the goods to their customers. Don't look for such fabrics at shopping mall fabric stores. There are a few specialized retailers in the country who carry them at full retail price, but in New York they can be found at substantial discounts.

These fabrics can be pricey, and even the bargains run into a bit of money, but if you compare the cost of clothes you make from these couture fabrics with prices in retail stores, you will appreciate the values.

The best bargains are in fabrics with distinctive patterns and colors. Designers rarely dispose of staples like black crepe de chine, but good fabric stores also buy directly from mills, so the staples are available.

▶ POLI FABRICS
132 WEST 57 STREET, BETWEEN SIXTH AND
SEVENTH AVENUES
(245-7589)

Not everything on Fifty-seventh Street is expensive. I once saw two well-dressed Italian customers at Poli's, buying yards and yards of Italian silk to be shipped to Italy. Why buy it here and not at home, I asked; "Because we cannot get it there at these prices," they said. Poli had been to the mills and bought their entire overstock, to be sold in the New York store at half the wholesale price.

There usually is a good selection of Harris tweed. Mohair coating from the Scaasi workroom (Barbara Bush's dressmaker) was $30 a yard the day I looked, and there is always wool jersey, Swiss cotton as fine as silk, and real silk jacquard for elegant blouses.

If you are lucky, you can make a Chanel suit in the same fabric that the Chanel designers used.

The hours are 9–6 M–Sa. Credit cards are not accepted here, but personal checks are and all sales are final.

A similar operation is:

▶ PARON FABRICS
With three stores:
60 WEST 57 STREET
(247-6451)
56 WEST 57 STREET, 2ND FLOOR
(247-6451)
239 WEST 39 STREET
(768-3266)

Prices are good at the street-level store on Fifty-seventh Street and extraordinary at the closeout store upstairs. On Thirty-ninth Street they have fabrics from both their other stores.

Management here will not disclose the names of their designer sources, but they are impeccable. You can find anything from embroidered lace for a ball gown and printed linen for a summer dress to fabrics suitable for couture-quality sportswear, all of natural fibers.

The hours in all stores are 9–6 M–Sa. Major credit cards are accepted and all sales are final.

On Thirty-ninth and Fortieth streets, between Seventh and Eighth avenues, there is one fabric store after another, and some have wonderful fabrics at bargain prices. Others are good stores for more prosaic needs—and some should be avoided because instead of bargains there is rude or totally inattentive personnel.

▶ B & J   FABRICS
263 WEST 40 STREET
(354-8150)

is a large store with three floors full of the best fabrics from all over the world, in natural fibers only—Liberty of London cottons and woolens, Moygashel linens, Viyella challis, wools and silks from other houses, Italian and French knits come from designers at end of season or directly from the mill. Mill closeouts are the best bargains, current styles are discounted 10 to 25 percent. There are also some fabrics for the home, like the Italian cotton tapestries for $20–$30 a yard. For evening wear or bridal gowns there is fabulous hand-beaded silk and lace.

The hours are 8–5:45 M–F, 9–4:45 Sa. Major credit cards are accepted and all sales are final.

▶ ART   MAX
250 WEST 40 STREET
(398-0744)

carries an international selection of fabrics from France, Switzerland, Japan, Italy, and elsewhere. Sometimes the selection is great and sometimes you will not find what you need, but it's worth strolling in.

The hours are 8–5:45 M–F, 9–5 Sa. Major credit cards are accepted and all sales are final.

▶ ROSEN AND CHADWICK
246 WEST 40 STREET
(869-0142)

The last time you saw a Broadway musical, the fabric for the costumes may have come from this large store. Their selection of theatrical fabrics is quite spectacular.

For non-theatrical wardrobes there are good end-of-season leftovers from Geoffrey Beene, Carolina Herrera, and other designers, as well as European imports from small mills in Italy, Scotland, and Switzerland. You will find Viyella challis, Swiss challis, Italian cotton and linen, many menswear fabrics and a lot more, often exclusive with this store.

The hours are 8:30–6 M–F, 9–5 Sa. Major credit cards are accepted and all sales are final.

▶ A & N FABRICS
268 WEST 39 STREET
(869-4081)

This is a discount store where you may find something that originally retailed for $70 a yard for $30, or a $5-a-yard cotton for $2. Besides the fabrics in the store, there is a big warehouse nearby and if you tell Harry Anderson what you need, he will go to the warehouse for you and show you samples of the available selection. He may also be able to duplicate a sample from a full-price fabric store at a discount of up to 30 percent. This kind of personal service is his strong point. Besides dress fabrics and suiting in natural fibers he carries the Japanese polyesters that feel like silk but wash like synthetics, and you can order Ultrasuede from him at a discount. There are also theatrical and bridal fabrics.

The hours are 9–6 M–F, 9–5 Sa. Major credit cards are accepted and all sales are final.

▶ A & K FABRICS
257 WEST 39 STREET
(944-5693)

This is a source for cotton, synthetics, denim, etc., from American mills and silk or polyester from Japan, at claimed discounts of 25 to 35 percent. Don't compare the quality with the Swiss cottons you have seen elsewhere, but come here when price matters more than haute-couture quality or when you want to make some denim skirts for yourself and your kids. Selection is good and the salespeople are very nice.

The hours are 9:30–6 M–F, 10–5 Sa. Major credit cards are accepted and all sales are final.

My reception at F & R and at C & F Fabrics on Thirty-ninth Street was so rude, I can recommend these stores only to shoppers with very thick skins; but why bother, when there are so many pleasant stores nearby?

FASHION KNITTING YARNS

▶ SMILEY'S YARNS
92–06 JAMAICA AVENUE (AT WOODHAVEN BLVD),
QUEENS
(718-849-9873)

If you can wait for their YARN RIOT! sale, which takes place approximately every three months, you can get fine imported yarns. Bernat, Pingoun, Tessand, Bouquet, and many other brands are available in great selection, packed in bags of ten or twelve balls—enough yarn to make a sweater. Half price is the most you will ever pay at these sales, but most of the time you will pay much less—discounts of 75 to 80 percent are not unusual here. The offerings are elegant first-quality yarns in a wide choice of colors, fibers, and textures, appropriate for the season. There is always some mohair, in the spring there are cottons and cotton/linen blends, and there usually is some baby yarn. I don't know how they can do it at these prices but they have been doing it for years and it's the best way to buy yarns—customers come from as far away as Pennsylvania for these bargains.

Call for the date of the next sale and travelling directions. Once you are on their mailing list, you will always be notified.

Hours are 10–5:30 M–Sa.

In Manhattan there is the:

▶ NEW YORK YARN CENTER
29 WEST 35 STREET
(594-9770)

The selection of closeouts here is outstanding. You may get yarn that would retail for $8 a skein for $3, or a $15 item for $7. There are Italian and French imports, and sometimes mohair and angora.

Besides closeouts, there are discounts on regular merchandise. Needles, instruction books, needlepoint yarns, and painted canvases are also sold here.

The hours are 10–6 M–F, 10–5 Sa, 12–5 Su. There is a minimum of $20 for major credit cards and store credit is given on returns within ninety days.

See also Truemart Fabrics in chapter 1, Garment Center Walking Tour.

MEN'S CLOTHING

Some men's suits retail for under $200; others for over $1,000. On a hanger they may both look good, but there are great differences in quality. Cheap prices don't always mean a bargain. Traditional tailoring techniques are labor-intensive and even good manufacturers use shortcuts that can be detrimental to the way a garment hangs and fits.

Interfacing gives a jacket its shape. If it is bonded (glued) rather than stitched in, this may present difficulties when alterations are needed and the bonding cannot be undone. If you wear jacket and tie only occasionally, top quality may not be important, but if that is your daily nine to five uniform, the best suit you can buy, within reason, will give you the best value in the long run.

The average men's suit takes three and a half yards of fabric that could cost as little as $5 a yard—or as much as $50—wholesale. The most expensive luxury fabric may not be the best value; cashmere, for instance, does not wear well, but a well-made suit of worsted wool or tweed will look and feel good for years, and may outlast a cheaper one.

Brands are an indication of quality, but reading the labels can also be very confusing: a good clothing factory may produce its own brand and also be a contractor for other labels which are of similar quality but not as well known. On the other hand, famous designer labels are often simply produced under license and one factory may do the tailoring for half a dozen designers. How can you tell? You can't—it's too complicated. Therefore, being label-conscious does not automatically make you an educated consumer. What's most important is that you learn to recognize quality when you see it, no matter what's on the label. You want really good fabric—usually 100 percent wool—but a small percentage of poly-ester in the blend can make a summer suit cooler and more wrin-kle-resistant. There is a certain feel to a fine piece of cloth, which you can learn only by comparing a cheap fabric to a good one in your hand. If you bunch a fabric up in your fist and then let go, the creases may stay in a poor fabric, but will be gone in a few minutes from a good one; a suit of that fabric will keep its press. Well-made buttonholes, substantial buttons sewn on securely, and a very smooth look at shoulders and lapels are important. Above all, never buy a jacket with telltale bubbles in the fabric. These are de-laminated spots where the bonding glue came undone, and a good pressing will not get rid of them.

If you wear a tuxedo more than once in two years, you will save money buying one. It's only twice the rental cost and has none of the rental inconvenience.

Custom tailors do not always stock fabrics; they carry sample books from which the customer can select the fabric for his suit. These merchant books, often very handsome, with leather covers, are issued by the people who supply the tailors with fabric, one suit at a time, at prices close to retail. This makes it possible to offer a vast selection, but the customer pays a lot for the service. Tailors who do enough business to buy their fabric in bolts have a tremendous price advantage: a quality fabric may cost $20 a yard wholesale, but the price for the same fabric in a sample book may be $60 a yard. A super deluxe fabric may wholesale for $50 a yard and cost as much as $200 a yard in a sample book. Since this practice does nothing at all for the quality of the suit, the smart customer will ask if there is any fabric in stock, and try to make his selection from that. However, since fabrics at wholesale have to be bought in large quantities, the best stock is kept by custom tailors who also produce ready-made suits in volume. This category includes Brooks Brothers and Saint Laurie.

▶ S Y M S

42 TRINITY PLACE (BETWEEN RECTOR STREET AND EXCHANGE PLACE)
(797-1199)

This store is where Syms began and where many of us found wonderful bargains: over-production and cancelled orders of well-known brands. Then it grew from one store into a nationwide chain with enormous buying power. There may not be enough quality over-production to supply so many stores, so now "things are seldom what they seem, skimmed milk masquerades as cream." This line from Gilbert and Sullivan's *HMS Pinafore* might describe the "bargains" here better than that empty phrase "An educated consumer is our best customer," which is repeated continuously in Syms' sales promotions.

Richard Behar, an investigative journalist who wrote a business story about Syms in *Forbes* magazine (September 9, 1985), exposed practices that make Syms a lot of money, while "sometimes hoodwinking those educated consumers." The article charges that you can find inferior merchandise with designer labels, made specially for Syms by less than scrupulous manufacturers, and made to sell for a lower price than their usual offerings. You may actually get exactly what you pay for, in spite of the label and the off-price claims.

Most of the offerings I saw didn't really seem to be top quality in fabric, cut, and workmanship. When I checked, there was a small selection of men's suits with labels by Givenchy, Sergio Valente, Portfolio, and Stanley Blacker, and many looked like tired rejects. More recently I heard of someone else's private label suits that were returned to the manufacturer because they were not first quality. I was told that they turned up at Syms, not identified as seconds, and priced higher than the other discounter's price for first quality.

The only quality bargains for men I saw, when I checked, were cashmere-blend socks marked "imperfect" for $5.95, claimed to retail for $17.50. There were also slacks, jackets, raincoats, all sorts of haberdashery, and shoes.

In the women's department, there were Bally shoes for $99 and Florsheim shoes for $39. There were a lot of jogging suits and some wool skirts by Schrader Sport, well priced but available only in pink. Cashmere sweaters from China with the SSSSSS house-brand label, a bit shopworn, were good buys at $39. Beautiful Scotty McGregor two-ply cashmere sweaters were outstanding bargains at $79 and $89, but there were only two on the floor.

Good bargains can be found here, but the educated consumer had better look for evident quality, not for labels.

The hours are 8–6:30 T, W, 8–7:30 Th, F, 10–6:30 Sa. Closed Sunday and Monday. Credit cards are not accepted and no refunds are given, but store credit is given within two weeks of purchase.

▶ S A I N T   L A U R I E   T A I L O R S
899 BROADWAY (AT 20TH STREET)
(473-0100)

Andrew Kozin is the third generation of his family to head Saint Laurie, a private-label producer of men's suits that are sold in good retail stores from coast to coast. Only in New York are these same suits offered directly to the public at considerable savings, in Saint Laurie's handsome building (which once was a Lord & Taylor store). Mr. Kozin's grandfather wanted only to become prosperous enough for his progeny to follow professional careers—which most of them did—but Andrew became fascinated with the romance of skilled craftsmanship and elected to continue the family's tailoring traditions.

Mr. Kozin and his associates are perfectionists. No matter how widespread the use of some tailoring shortcut, you will not find it practiced here: interfacings are layered and stitched instead of glued or bonded, waistbands are made in a labor-intensive way that makes them give when the wearer sits down, and buttons and buttonholes are sewn with time-honored techniques. Patterns are drafted on a computer, because it's more accurate than doing it the old way.

Visitors are encouraged to take a self-guided tour through the building and learn what goes into the construction of a well-tailored garment; groups can arrange to take a guided tour.

Any suit on the rack can be ordered in any other fabric from their extensive collection, with delivery in four to six weeks. Men's styles range from a traditional English cut with natural shoulders to a sharp contemporary European look with wider shoulders and a closer-fitting jacket. The price range is $400–$600 for a man's or woman's suit. This is claimed to be a third less than the retail price for the same garments elsewhere.

The designer here is Alphonse Abbate, who used to design Saks Fifth Avenue's private label suits until Saks stopped making them.

Mr. Abbate also presides over the custom tailoring department. Suits here cost $700–$1200 depending on fabric. Those made from Saint Laurie's own stock of fabrics are by far the best value, but other sample books can be inspected for a wider selection.

Some people need custom tailoring for a perfect fit, but most can be fitted with one of the many off-the-rack sizes. Alterations are done free of charge by arrangement with Marsan Tailors, an independent alteration shop which is a tenant in the Saint Laurie building.

Another tenant is Carlton Weavers, who can repair moth holes or cigarette burns invisibly, in many kinds of fabric.

Private-label shirts of 100 percent cotton are priced from $40–$80 (the top price is for Sea Island cotton). The same shirt that costs $69 here can sell on Fifth Avenue, with another label, for $90–110.

There are sales every January and June, and a big warehouse sale every February, when prices are further reduced.

The hours are 9:30–6 M, T, W, Sa, 9:30–7:30 Th, 12–5 Su. Closed

Sunday in July and August and closed for vacation the last week of July and the first week of August. Major credit cards are accepted and refunds given within two weeks of purchase.

Saint Laurie suits for women are described in chapter 6.

▶ M O E   G I N S B E R G
162 FIFTH AVENUE
(982-5254)

There really is a Moe Ginsberg, and his personality dominates three large floors in a loft building, where he does business. I have been told that departing customers who have not made a purchase are sometimes treated to a few insults by Mr. Ginsberg himself.

Since the neighborhood is becoming gentrified and designer boutiques are lining Fifth Avenue at street level, he would now like to create an upscale image, so he and his son refused to be interviewed for a book that deals with bargains. The clothes still hang on pipe racks and there is a minimalist decor of bare floors and fluorescent lighting. If money is no object, the street-floor designer boutiques and nearby Barney's have much more elegant settings.

Image or not, one can find good bargains here, like the Hathaway cotton shirts and the suits by Stanley Blacker, which sell well below the retail price. It's a big operation and still growing (the latest addition is a shoe department), so they must be doing something right.

Open seven days a week: 9:30–7 M–F, 9:30–8 Sa, 9:30–6 Su. Major credit cards are accepted.

▶ B F O
149 FIFTH AVENUE (AT 21ST STREET), 6TH FLOOR
(254-0059)

A few years ago, there was not much to interest sophisticated shoppers here, but with a change of management things have changed a lot. Clothes from the best American and European factories are sold here now, with well-known as well as obscure labels (see the introduction to this chapter) at discounts that are claimed to be close to 50 percent. There are seven BFO stores in the New York area (the other six are in Yonkers; Carle Place, L.I.; Princeton, N.J.; Union, N.J.; Clifton, N.J.; and Norwalk, Conn.) and they are affiliated with thirteen Gentry stores in the midwest. That accounts for the good prices: a twenty-store chain has buying power! Suits, jackets, slacks, raincoats, overcoats, and tuxedos in sizes 36–52 S, R, L, XS, XL, Portly, and Portly Short are sold here. Everything is first-quality, current merchandise and fast alterations are available on the premises. The store caters to visitors from out of town and delivers to hotels or via UPS to the customer's home anywhere in the U.S. There are frequent sales throughout the year, which are advertised in the newspapers, or you can call the store for the date of their next sale. The big annual warehouse sale that runs two weeks before and one week after Labor Day has the best bargains.

The hours are 9:30–6, seven days a week except M and Th, when they are 9:30–7. Major credit cards and personal checks are accepted. Refunds are given within thirty days of purchase. Bring this book to the store and get an additional $20 off on a suit.

▶ BFO PLUS
(SAME ADDRESS AS ABOVE)
(673-9026)

The separate salesroom on the second floor is an excellent source of haberdashery. The prices for dress shirts and silk ties are among the lowest I have seen, but these are not closeouts, so the selection is comprehensive. Every man should have a few drip-dry dress shirts for travel and for the day the laundry lets him down; for 100% cotton shirts he can choose among the selection here, which includes Pima and Sea Island cotton. Sizes range from 14½ neck, 32 sleeve to 18 neck, 36 sleeve, in full cut and fitted styles. There are also sports shirts and very good sweaters, including some of two-ply cashmere. Slacks, jeans, belts, down jackets, socks, under-wear, gloves, and scarves complete the assortment. Silk neckties with designer labels are displayed along one whole wall, priced from $9.50 to $18. They would cost as much as $60 at full retail.

All merchandise is first quality and styles are current. Discounts are claimed to be 30 to 50 percent. Sale dates are the same as at BFO upstairs. Major credit cards are accepted with a $20 mini-mum.

Note: BFO and BFO Plus are negotiating for a street-level loca-tion on lower Fifth Avenue. The plan was to combine both stores in 1991. Before you go, telephone and verify the address.

▶ D A F F Y ' S
III FIFTH AVENUE
(529-4477)

335 MADISON AVENUE
(557-4422)

The men's department on the lower floor of this discount cloth-ing store has many good bargains in suits, overcoats, raincoats, sportswear, dress and sports shirts, underwear, and more. Casual clothes come in conservative as well as very trendy styles. Calvin Klein, Adolfo, Damiani, Praino, and Kinniku are among the de-signers you will find here. Sweaters are by Joseph About, leather fashions by Phillip Monet, ties by Hugo Boss and Modules, and occasionally there are sample shoes. Discounts range from 25 to 50 percent, but there are progressive reductions and continual clearance sales, so you could find something you want for even less.

The store hours are 10–9 M–Sa, 11–6 Su. Visa and MasterCard are accepted and purchases can be returned within seven days for store credit.

▶ R O T H M A N ' S
200 PARK AVENUE SOUTH (AT 17TH STREET)
(777-7400)

Before they moved to this spiffy new store a couple of years ago,
Rothman's had been on lower Fifth Avenue for generations, catering to many thrifty celebrities whose handwritten letters were
prominently displayed. The new store practices more discretion,
but well-known actors and athletes are still among their regular
customers.

Some very exclusive and expensive brands are sold at discounts
that are claimed to be 30 to 60 percent and the management here
quoted brand names for the record: Hickey-Freeman, Norman Hilton, Perry Ellis and Alexander Julian suits, Sanyo and Drizzle raincoats, Kenneth Gordon shirts and sweaters, Aquascutum ties.
Norman Hilton has a warehouse sale once a year in their New
Jersey factory, but Rothman's prices on first-quality Norman Hilton
suits are claimed to be lower all year round. The selection of styles
and sizes is excellent and all merchandise is first quality and current.

Open seven days a week, 10–7 M–F, 10–8 Th, 9–6 Sa, 12–5 Su.
Major credit cards are accepted and refunds given within ten days
of purchase.

Bring a copy of this book, buy any suit, and get a free silk tie.

▶ D O L L A R   B I L L ' S
99 EAST 42 STREET
(867-0212)

880 THIRD AVENUE

The clothes here come from Italy and are closeouts, cancelled
orders, and last season's leftovers from European factories and
retail stores. This means that what you find here may or may not
be current merchandise and may or may not be available in your
size. I have seen suits and raincoats by one of Italy's top designers

at bargain prices, and a lot of lesser offerings, including domestic shirts and ties that did not strike me as great bargains. Discounts are claimed to be 10 to 80 percent. Some of the bargains are spectacular, but you must understand quality to find them.

The women's department, up a flight of stairs, has more Italian designers, including the famous ones, often at bargain prices.

The hours are 8–7 M–F, 10–6 Sa. Major credit cards are accepted, refunds given within seven days of purchase, and store credit given within fourteen days.

▶ LS MEN'S CLOTHING
19 WEST 44 STREET, ROOM 403
(575-0933)

Samples, overproduction, cancellations, and clearly marked, slightly imperfect men's clothing from the very best American sources are sold in this no-frills, upstairs store at 40 to 60 percent discounts. H. Freeman, Ralph Lauren, and DAKS, as well as other famous brands that cannot be mentioned in print, are offered in a wide selection of sizes and styles. Raincoats are imported from Japan and overcoats from Canada, both from impeccable sources.

Merchandise is current and, unless labeled imperfect, it is first quality. There are thousands of garments on the racks, but if you don't find what you want in your size, it can usually be ordered at a slightly higher price. In-stock suits are priced from $185 to $425, this for a suit that usually retails for $875.

Sizes include 36 S–52 XL as well as Portly, Portly Short, Cadet and Tall Cadet, but people who need unusual sizes should call before they come. The management here is very service-oriented, so it is not surprising that many senior executives who are used to good service are steady customers, because they appreciate a bargain. This is also a good source for tuxedos. Alterations are done on the premises.

The hours are 9–7 M–Th, 9–4 F, 10–5 Su. Major credit cards are accepted and delivery via UPS is available.

▶ EXPLORER'S COMPANY AND LEWIS AND CLARK

The stores in this small chain are under separate managements, but they pool their buying power so they can sell casual men's clothing at 35 to 65 percent discounts. Slacks, jackets, dress and sport shirts, sweaters, coats, leather clothes, outerwear, and accessories all come with good brand names which I have been asked not to mention in print. The clothes are casual and conservative—what the well-dressed man wears on weekends. Lots of women have discovered the values here and come for their own sweaters, shirts, and raincoats. The stores are:

EXPLORER'S COMPANY
228 SEVENTH AVENUE (23RD ST.) (255-4686)

EXPLORER'S COMPANY
27 SEVENTH AVENUE (12TH ST.) (255-2322)

EXPLORER'S COMPANY
115 WEST BROADWAY (BETWEEN DUANE AND READE) (406-9575)

LEWIS AND CLARK
591 BROADWAY (BETWEEN PRINCE AND HOUSTON) (226-9277)

LEWIS AND CLARK
751 BROADWAY (BETWEEN 8TH ST. AND ASTOR PLACE) (254-6534)

All stores take major credit cards and give refunds within ten days of purchase. *All are open seven days a week, 11–7 M–F, 11–6 Sa, 12–5 Su.*

▶ VICTORY SHIRTS
485 MADISON AVENUE
(753-1679)

The downtown branch of this store is described on the Orchard Street Walking Tour, but the hours here are different: *9–7 M–F, 9–6 Sa.*

▶ WALLACH'S WAREHOUSE
3100 47TH AVENUE, LONG ISLAND CITY
(718-482-8442)

Wonderful bargains can be found in this outlet for Hartmarx, a manufacturer of men's and women's suits, and for a chain of retail stores owned by Hartmarx, which include Wallach's and Tripler. There is a vast selection of clothes for men and women, haberdashery, and blouses, all more than 50 percent below retail. Men's shoes include expensive brands like Bally, Salvatore Ferragamo, and Cole-Haan. They sell out fast, because they never cost more than $99. Shoes for women are not available.

This is a basic warehouse operation, so there are no fitting rooms or alterations.

The hours are 11–8 W–F, 10–5 Sa, 12–5 Su. Major credit cards are accepted and store credit given within 30 days of purchase.

To get there by subway, take the #7 Flushing line from Grand Central to 33rd Street. Take the 33rd Street exit and walk one block against traffic to 47th Avenue.

▶ FOWAD
2554 BROADWAY (AT 96TH ST)
(222-5000)

The men's department at this bargain outlet carries shirts, trousers, jackets, suits, outerwear, raincoats, ties, and socks, with labels like Pierre Cardin, John Henry, and Cotler. Sixty-nine dollars is usually the highest price here for any item, with brand-name shirts selling for $6.99 and $8.99.

They are open from 9:30–7:30 M–Sa, 11–5 Su. Major credit cards are accepted and refunds given within three days of purchase.

FOR TALL AND BIG MEN:

▶ JOSEPH M. KLEIN
118 STANTON STREET
(228-1166)

No need to pay a premium for large sizes. Clothes from size 40 to 74, shirts from 15½ to 22 with sleeves to 38″ are discounted here at a claimed 25 to 30 percent. Members Only, Career Club, Halston, and Pierre Cardin are among the brands that can be found.

This store is open seven days a week, 9:30–6 M–Sa, 9:30–5 Su. Major credit cards are accepted and store credit given within ten days of purchase.

See chapter 2, Lower Manhattan Walking Tour for: Louis Barrall and Son, Gorsart, and Young Hats.

See chapter 3, Orchard Street Walking Tour for: The Europa Collection, Tobaldi Huomo, Antony, Victory Shirts, S. Sosinsky, G&G International, Penn Garden, Euro Moda, and Pan Am Men's Clothing.

For more custom tailors, see chapter 5, Chinatown Walking Tour.

SHOES FOR MEN
AND WOMEN

▶ RETAIL SHOE OUTLET
537 BROADWAY (BETWEEN PRINCE AND SPRING STREETS)
(966-4070)

It seems unreal: Salvatore Ferragamo, I. Miller, Palizzio, Saks Fifth Avenue, and many other brands of good leather shoes share shelf space—and prices—with stiff-as-a-board cheap vinyl shoes and better-quality manmade trendies. Nothing is over $35, and the second pair you buy is always half price.

This shop is affiliated with Shoe Town, a chain of discount shoe outlets. They send their odds and ends, returns, broken lots, etc., here, where the object seems to be to dispose of them at any price. People who come here often tell tales of Delman evening slippers for $3, Saks storm boots for $5, Italian suede pumps for $7. What you find may be an unusual style or color, or out-of-season merchandise, so come with an open mind and be prepared to do some impulse buying. On a recent visit I bought a stylish pair of light blue Ferragamo flats, white and beige leather Chanel-style pumps, teal blue walking shoes with red rubber soles, and rugged walking shoes of oiled leather with heavy crepe soles. I got change for $50. I did not find the navy pumps I really needed, but how could I resist the other goodies, at this price?

The neighborhood is becoming gentrified and prices are going up, but so is the selection of better-quality merchandise. Top price for leather boots was $80 last year, with drastic reductions at the end of the season.

Top quality men's leather shoes with leather linings and soles were $80 when I looked, but you can do well here for $40, and there are also men's boots and athletic shoes.

The hours are 9–6 M–F, 9–5 Sa, 10–6 Su. Visa and MasterCard are accepted and all sales are final.

A similar store is

▶ SHOE GIANT
166—25 JAMAICA AVENUE, QUEENS
(718-658-5056)

▶ GUCCI ON SEVEN
45 ENTERPRISE AVENUE NORTH, SECAUCUS, N.J.
(201-867-8800)

Gucci stores are too upscale to have sales, so they send all their sale merchandise to this store. The name refers to the fact that it used to be on the seventh floor above the Gucci store on Fifth Avenue, until it moved to larger quarters in Secaucus.

Here you will find the famous Gucci shoes reduced by a claimed 30 to 75 percent. They do not fit every foot because they are made on a narrow last, but some people who spend a lot of time on their feet will not wear anything else because they find the Guccis so comfortable. The store also carries handbags, luggage, scarves, accessories, and sportswear for men and women.

I am sorry to report that I found Gucci's reputation for rude service entirely justified here. *The hours are 10–9 Th, 12–5 Su, 10–6 all other days.* Major credit cards are accepted and refunds given within 10 days of purchase.

BALLY OUTLETS

▶ HARMON COVE OUTLET CENTER
20 ENTERPRISE AVENUE N, SECAUCUS, N.J.
(201-864-3444)

I BALLY PLACE, NEW ROCHELLE
(914-632-4444)

See the foreword for traveling directions to Harmon Cove, which is in walking distance of this store.

The expensive shoes from Switzerland are sold in the company's own outlet stores for a claimed discount of 25 to 60 percent. Some are current styles and some are from previous seasons, but all are first-quality merchandise and selection is good.

Men's shoes come in sizes 5–15, women's in 4–11 N, M, and occasionally W. There are also elegant tailored handbags, briefcases, and attachés.

The hours in Secaucus are 10–6 M–W, Sa, 10–9 Th, F, 12–5 Su.

The hours in New Rochelle are 10–8 M–F, 10–6 Sa, 12–5 Su. The Bally building is across the street from the railway station and has a giant sign on the roof, so it's not hard to find. By car, take Route 95 north to exit 16, turn left at the stop sign, then take the first right turn you come to.

There are other Bally outlets in Philadelphia and Orlando, Florida.

Sometimes finding shoes that fit and look good can be a problem at any price. If you have hard-to-fit feet you may be willing to forego discounts in favor of selection.

▶ HILL BROTHERS SHOES
99 NINTH STREET, LYNCHBURG VIRGINIA 24504
(804-528-1000)

This catalogue offers women's shoes in sizes 2–14, widths AAAAA–EEEE. Styles include plain leather pumps in many colors and several heel heights, flats, evening shoes, sneakers, and leather boots. You don't need to worry about fit, because the firm has a very liberal return policy: if they hurt, send them back, even if you have worn them in the street. Not every style is available in every size, but selection is good and prices are moderate—nothing is over $70. Both leather and better-quality vinyl are shown (it's good to own at least one vinyl pair to wear in the rain—they are indestructible). At these prices you will not find the finest leather shoes with leather linings and soles, but many of these shoes look and feel good, and if you wear a hard-to-find size, this catalogue will broaden your shoe horizon.

UNUSUAL SIZES FOR MEN

▶ HITCHCOCK SHOES
165 BEAL STREET, HINGHAM, MASSACHUSETTS 02043
(617-749-3571)

Write for their catalogue.

CUSTOM-MADE SHOES FOR MEN AND WOMEN

▶ LILLIE SHOE COMPANY
PENINSULA HOTEL, KOWLOON, HONG KONG

You don't have to travel to Hong Kong because Mr. Wong makes a tour of the U.S. twice a year to show his samples and take orders. Your feet will be measured when you place your first order and individual lasts will be made and kept at the factory in Hong Kong, to be used for future orders. Styles are chic, high-quality calfskin is available in many colors (snake, lizard, and alligator are also available), and of course these shoes are leather-lined and have leather soles, like the best handmade shoes from Europe. Hong Kong prices have gone up in the last few years, but if you have a fitting problem or can't find styles you like in your size, these shoes will cost much less than custom-made shoes from anywhere else. Write and ask to be put on the mailing list, and you will be invited to visit Mr. Wong's hotel suite the next time he is in town.

SEE ALSO

Shoe Steal, Anbar, and Shoe Gallery on the Lower Manhattan Walking Tour; Trevi, Sole of Italy, Lace Up, Orchard Bootery, Accessories Arcade, and J. Sherman on the Orchard Street Walking Tour; Shoe Repair, Leslie's Bootery, and M & M Shoe Center on the Grand Street tour.

ATHLETIC SHOES

► CARLSON IMPORTS
524 BROADWAY (AT SPRING STREET)
(431-5940)

This wholesaler of athletic shoes for men, women, and children sells to the public in a Soho loft showroom, at prices that are claimed to be 15 to 50 percent below retail. The selection will suit the Sunday walker as well as the basketball star; brands include Adidas, Puma, Nike, Reebok, Etonic, Brooks, Asics Tiger, Kangaroo, New Balance, Converse, and Patrick. Sizes go from infant all the way to a man's size 17.

You will also find a selection of sweat socks and warmup suits here.

The hours are 9–5 M–F, 9–4:30 Sa, 11–4:30 Su. Credit cards are not accepted, personal checks with ID are welcome, and refunds are given within thirty days of purchase.

LINGERIE AND UNDERWEAR

▶ **UNDERWEAR PLAZA**
1421 62 STREET, BROOKLYN
(718-232-6804)

These people are wholesalers of lingerie closeouts, who supply Filene's Basement, Marshall's, and similar stores with well-known brands. Dior, Eve Stillman, Calvin Klein, Kayser, Vassarette, Bali bras and similar brands are carried, and discounts are claimed to be at least 50 percent.

Come for a four-pack of panties that usually retail for $4–$8 each, and pay $10 for the lot, or come for elegant, trousseau-quality peignoir sets, silk teddies, and other luxuries. Hard-to-find large sizes are carried in foundation garments as well as lingerie, and everything can be tried on in a fitting room. Selection in all categories is excellent. When I looked, three pairs of first quality Evan-Picone pantyhose were sold for the price of one and Natori slippers for a claimed discount of 60 percent.

The hours are: 10–5 Su–Th, 10–2 F. Major credit cards and personal checks are accepted and all sales are final.

► BARBIZON OUTLET
HARMON COVE OUTLET CENTER, SECAUCUS, N.J.
(201-867-1714)

This is one of a number of outlets owned and run by the people
who make the pretty embroidered cotton lingerie and sleep wear.
Nightgowns that cost over $40 at department stores and around
$25 or more at discounters have been found here for $10. If you
are a Barbizon fan, the savings are worth a trip.

There is also a Barbizon outlet at:

► FEED MILL PLAZA
FLEMINGTON, N.J.
(201-806-4653)

SEE ALSO

Kaufman, Schachner, Mendel Weiss, Louis Chock, Goldman and
Cohen, and D & A on the Orchard Street Walking Tour. See Imkar
and Mayfield on the Grand Street Walking Tour and Century 21
on the Lower Manhattan Walking Tour.

EVERYTHING FOR KIDS

CLOTHES

▶ DAFFY'S
III FIFTH AVENUE (AT 18TH STREET)
(529-4477)

335 MADISON AVENUE (AT 44TH STREET)
(557-4422)

The children's department of this large fashion discounter has quality bargains for kids from infants to size 14 for girls, size 20 for boys. The stock changes constantly, so you can never be sure what you will find when you come, but even if you have to come more than once, it may be worth the effort, because they carry some very good brands, and discounts are claimed to be a minimum of 50 percent.

Dior for Kids, Deux par deux, Magid dresses, Choosey, Sweet Potato, Lemur, Le Chat, Babymini, and David Charles dresses are among the designer brands you will find here. Daffy's in Paramus also carries Polo for Boys and Arturo.

For other descriptions of Daffy's, see chapter 11 on men's clothing and chapter 6, women's fashions.

▶ CONWAY STORES
1333 BROADWAY (AT 36TH STREET) AND OTHER
LOCATIONS
(967-3460)

This is rough-duty shopping: narrow aisles, crowds, merchandise piled on tables; you dig through mountains of prosaic stuff to find the goodies, and find them you will.

I have bought 100 percent cotton sunsuits with matching sun hats here and sent them to the mothers of well-dressed tots in upscale suburbs; all the other moms wanted to know where these cute outfits came from for which I had paid a whole $3.95.

Merchandise consists of closeouts and cancelled orders; it is impossible to speak in terms of discounts, because prices are often way below the wholesale price. Both well-known American brands and unknown imports are carried, but you never know what you will find, because the stock changes constantly. The stores also carry men's and women's clothing, handbags, bed and bath items, and health and beauty aids, but on my infrequent visits the children's clothes have always been outstanding. The following Conway stores have children's departments:

1333 BROADWAY	243 WEST 34 ST
225 WEST 35 ST	450 SEVENTH AVENUE
11 WEST 34 ST	37 BROAD STREET

Other Conway stores are at:

49 WEST 34 STREET	41 BROAD STREET
1345 BROADWAY	247 WEST 34 STREET
251 WEST 34 STREET	

The hours in all stores are 8–7:30 M–Sa, 11–6 Su. Major credit cards are accepted and refunds are given within twenty-five days of purchase.

▶ SECOND COUSIN
142 SEVENTH AVENUE (AT 10TH STREET)
(929-8048)

Popular brands like Oshkosh, all-cotton legging sets and underwear sets from Japan, baby carriers, Jolly Jumpers, Sesame Street toys, and other cute things are discounted 20 percent here. This is new merchandise. The store also carries gently worn, used children's clothes (see chapter 26).

Open 11–7 M–Sa. Major credit cards are accepted and store credit given within two weeks.

▶ NATHAN BORLAM
157 HAVEMEYER STREET, BROOKLYN
(718-387-2983)

People who were taken here as children to buy clothes now bring their own grandchildren for quality bargains. Sizes range from infant to pre-teen, and discounts are claimed to be from 30 to 50 percent. There are well-known American and European brands, as well as a good deal of private-label merchandise, which was made by contractors who also work for big-name designers like Pierre Cardin and Ralph Lauren. Mr. Borlam claims that his boys' dress suits are made of the finest worsted wool of similar or better quality than what is used in designer-label clothes. Blazers, sports jackets, and suits come in Regular, Slim, and Husky sizes and there are also lots of casual boys' clothes, including three-quarter down coats in many colors. For girls there are lots of trendy casual clothes, pretty party dresses, down jackets, and wool coats. Lucky kids that take winter vacations in warm climates will find beach attire here the year round. Families with several kids make pilgrimages here, because they can really save money; the prices are often the very best in the city.

The store is not far from Manhattan—just across the Williamsburg bridge. To come by subway, go to the Marcy Avenue stop on the #7 Flushing line. By car, take the Brooklyn Queens Expressway to the Metropolitan Avenue exit, which is near the store's own parking lot.

The hours are 10–6 Su–Th, 10–2 F. Credit cards are not accepted, but personal checks are and refunds are given within eight days of purchase.

► FAMOUS BRANDS FACTORY OUTLET
168 39 STREET, BROOKLYN
(718-788-3158)

Take the B, N, or R train to the 36th Street stop and walk to the factory that produces a very famous brand of infants' and children's clothes, which I cannot mention in print; this is the factory store. They sell merchandise from other brands as well, so you can find complete layettes, quilted patchwork bedding, chic outerwear, and a variety of clothes up to size 14, all at discounts of 30 to 60 percent.

The hours are 10–3 M–Th, 10–12 F. Major credit cards are accepted and all sales are final.

► FOWAD
2554 BROADWAY (AT 96TH ST)
(222-5000)

This closeout store is described in chapter 6: Women's Fashions. Although they do not have a children's department, they do sell children's clothes from time to time, at rock-bottom closeout prices.

CHILDREN'S SHOES

▶ RICHIE'S DISCOUNT
CHILDREN'S SHOES
783 AVENUE B (BETWEEN 11TH AND 12TH STREETS)
(228-5442)

On the same spot for eighty-three years, Richie's has served generations of customers and still does it graciously and economically. They are almost fanatical about fit. If they think your child does not need new shoes, they will send you home without them. Mr. Richie suggests you call before you come and tell him what you need, to make sure a good selection is available. All good brands, in sizes from infants to a teenage size 8, are sold at discounts of 10 to 50 percent.

Twice every year, in November and from May 15–June 15, there is a major sale, when many good shoes sell for just $10 a pair.

Visa and MasterCard are accepted and refunds given within thirty days.

The hours are 10–5 every day except Wednesday.

▶ RAGAZZINI
37—15 30 AVENUE (NEAR STEINWAY STREET), ASTORIA,
QUEENS
(718-278-4221)

This store imports children's shoes directly from Italy, Spain, and Greece. Quality and fashion are exceptional—well worth the trip to Astoria. The shoes are beautifully made of 100 percent leather (including soles and lining), and I was told that they are constructed in an anatomically correct way to prevent fallen arches and other foot problems. Styles and colors are very fashionable and can be compared to what one finds in an upscale children's boutique, but here the prices are lower. When I looked, they were $30–$50, depending on size. Sizes are from infants to an adult size 8, of which they sell more to mommies than to kids; where else can you find a fashionable pair of 100 percent leather flats for $50?

The store is open 7 days a week from 10–7 except Sunday, when the hours are 12–5. Visa and MasterCard are accepted and store credit given within ten days of purchase.

SEE ALSO

A&G, Tobaldini, Trevi (shoes), and Louis Chock (layettes) on the Orchard Street Walking Tour, Rice and Breskin and M. Kreiner, on the Grand Street Walking Tour, and Kid's Town on the Lower Manhattan Walking Tour.

TOYS

▶ THE RED CABOOSE
16 WEST 45 STREET, 4TH FLOOR
(575-0155)

Train buffs of all ages come here for their trains, scenery, and buildings. They can buy anything from a tiny Z-gauge train to a LGB giant train from Germany. Collectors will find old Lionel trains that are no longer in production, and beginners can get a starter set for $65. Discounts are claimed to be 10 to 30 percent.

The hours are 10–7 M–F, 10–5:30 Sa. Major credit cards are accepted and store credit given indefinitely.

▶ HERSHEY STATIONERY AND TOYS
48 CLINTON STREET
(473-6391)

The store's owner has been at this spot for fifty years and has seen many changes in the neighborhood. Located between Stanton and

Rivington streets in what is now the Hispanic Lower East Side, Mr. Hershey still sells popular toys by Playschool, Fisher-Price, Mattell, and Hasbro at discounts claimed to be 20 to 25 percent. *The hours are 10–5 Su–F.* Credit cards and checks are not accepted and all sales are final.

FURNITURE FOR KIDS

▶ **BEN'S BABYLAND**
87 AVENUE A (BETWEEN 5TH AND 6TH STREETS)
(674-1353)

Cribs by Simmons, carriages by Baby Trend, Baby B, and others, nursery furniture, toys, swings, gates, and other safety items are discounted here 20 to 40 percent. Selection and service are excellent.

The hours are 10–5, seven days a week. MasterCard and Visa are accepted and refunds given within fourteen days of purchase.

▶ **ALBEE BABY CARRIAGES, INC.**
715 AMSTERDAM AVENUE (AT 95TH STREET)
(662-5740)

Here you will find a good selection of layettes, cribs, bedding, carriages, strollers, gates, high chairs, playpens, walkers, and toys for children up to age four, discounted a claimed 10 to 20 percent. The store takes mail or phone orders and ships to customers coast to coast. *In New York the hours are 9–5 M–Sa.* Major credit cards are accepted and refunds given with thirty days of purchase.

LUGGAGE

What kind of luggage should you get? It depends on the kind of traveling you do. There is very little difference in appearance between cheap and more expensive luggage—the difference is in the construction and in the amount of wear a piece of luggage will take gracefully. If you travel only occasionally and then by car, you may not need luggage that can take rough handling. If your luggage will be tumbling down airport carousels on a regular basis, spend more for the best—it will pay in the long run and you will never find yourself far from home with a broken lock or handle.

So-called designer luggage is often handsome, but not always of the best quality and not a really good buy. The luggage manufacturer must pay a hefty licensing fee to use the designer's name and that is reflected in the price. Often this luggage is sold only in sets, which sounds good, until you discover that there are pieces in the set which you never use.

Fortunately, good luggage can be bought at very substantial discounts in several stores around town:

► LEXINGTON LUGGAGE
793 LEXINGTON AVENUE
(223-0698) OR (800-822-0404)

Boyt, Andiamo, Tumi, Samsonite, American Tourister, and London Fog's soft luggage are the brands recommended here, but others are carried as well. Since their volume is very big, they are able to work on a small profit margin—10 percent over wholesale. This means that prices are usually 40 percent below retail, but when the manufacturer offers a special promotion, the price can be as much as 50 percent off. You can always find the newest innovations here, like self-healing nylon fabric covers and the Boyt "walk-in closet," a carry-on bag with room to hang clothes and space for shirts, shoes, toilet kits, etc. It never needs to be unpacked, which is wonderful when you stay in a different place each night.

Lexington stocks 90 percent of the lines they carry, so you can usually find the size and color you want. They also have a good selection of briefcases, attaché cases, and small leather goods for immediate delivery. Monogramming is free, and so is delivery in Manhattan.

The hours are 9–6:30, M–Sa. Major credit cards are accepted and refunds given within thirty days of purchase, provided the piece has not been used or monogrammed. They ship anywhere.

► JOBSON LUGGAGE
666 LEXINGTON AVENUE (AT 55 STREET)
(355-6846) OR FOR ORDERS OUTSIDE OF NEW YORK CITY
(800-221-5238)

The selection here includes most major brands—Samsonite, Lucas, Andiamo, Boyt, Tumi, Ventura, Skyway, Lark, and Halliburton are stocked—as well as all sorts of small leather goods, briefcases, and attaché cases. What's not in stock can be ordered. Free monogramming is available and discounts are claimed to be 40 to 50 percent, which is only 10 percent above their cost.

The hours are 9–6 M–Sa. Major credit cards are accepted and refunds given within thirty days of purchase for unused merchandise that has not been monogrammed.

► ROMANO TRADING
628 WEST 45 STREET
(581-4248)

This store is better-known in France and Italy than in New York —it has been profiled on television in both countries. Originally the location was chosen to serve the people who work on ships in New York harbor. Few ships dock here nowadays, but Romano's store is still well-known in Europe and getting well-known in New York for excellent prices. They carry Samsonite, Ventura, and Halliburton luggage at a claimed 45 to 50 percent discount, and they also carry brand-name linens, Parker pens, Prince tennis rackets, Ray-Ban sunglasses, Dior umbrellas, Seiko watches, and a great many other things at discounts that make a trip to the western shore of Manhattan worthwhile.

The hours are 8:30–5 M–F, 9–4 Sa.

SEE ALSO:

Bettinger Luggage on the Orchard Street tour and Luggage Plus on the Grand Street tour.

FURNITURE

When you buy furniture from a dealer, you are often only ordering the furniture for future delivery, weeks or months from the day you place the order. In New York City the law requires that a delivery date be specified on the order form. If it cannot be met, the dealer is required to inform you in writing. He then has another thirty days to make delivery. After that, you may cancel the order and receive a full refund (the dealer is not permitted to charge a cancellation fee) or you can agree to a new delivery date. These regulations, as well as other useful advice, are explained in a free brochure from the

NEW YORK CITY DEPARTMENT OF CONSUMER AFFAIRS
80 LAFAYETTE STREET, NEW YORK, NY 10013 (577-0111)

When your new furniture is delivered, you will be asked to sign for it. If you have not had time to thoroughly inspect it before you are asked for your signature, write "subject to inspection" on the receipt and report any defects as soon as you find them. Don't accept delivery of partial orders: if you ordered eight dining chairs and only three are delivered, you will really be stuck if the rest never come. Styles do get discontinued and the factory is not going to cut five chairs just for you.

FURNITURE CLEARANCE CENTERS

All the department stores that sell furniture and many better furniture stores maintain large furniture clearance centers. What you will find there is the new furniture that has been refused because of late delivery, cancelled special orders, as well as floor samples, mistakes (wrong finish, wrong fabric, etc.), and slightly soiled or scratched pieces. They are sold "as is" at big discounts. One other advantage of shopping in a clearance center is the fact that your furniture is available for immediate delivery. Often there are also rugs, bedding, and appliances such as TV sets and microwave ovens—and sometimes even refrigerators.

MACY'S CLEARANCE CENTER
ROUTE 22, SPRINGFIELD, N.J.
(201-376-8698)

Open 10–9 M-Sa.

MACY'S CLEARANCE CENTER
174 GLEN COVE ROAD, CARLE PLACE, L.I.
(516-746-1490)

Open 10–9:30 M-Sa.

MACY'S CLEARANCE CENTER
425 NORTH CENTRAL AVENUE, HARTSDALE
(914-761-7771)

Open 10–9 M–F, 10–5:30 Sa, 12–5:30 Su.

Macy's charge card and major credit cards are accepted at all centers, and all sales are final. Discounts are claimed to be approximately 25 percent of the prices charged in Macy's stores.

► A & S CLEARANCE CENTER
155 GLEN COVE ROAD, CARLE PLACE, L.I.
(516-742-8500)

Open 11–9:30 M-Sa, 12–5:30 Su.

A & S charge cards, Visa, and MasterCard are accepted, and all sales are final. In the same building is:

► BLOOMINGDALE'S CLEARANCE CENTER
155 GLEN COVE ROAD, CARLE PLACE, L.I.
(516-248-1400)

Discounts are claimed to be 20 to 70 percent here. Ther are some seconds, but flaws are clearly marked on the ticket.

Open 10–9:30 M-F, 10–6 Sa, 12–5 Su.

Bloomingdale's charge cards and major credit cards are accepted, and all sales are final.

► CASTRO CONVERTIBLES CLEARANCE CENTER
1990 JERICHO TURNPIKE, NEW HYDE PARK, L.I.
(516-488-3000)

Showroom samples and returns are sold here at claimed discounts of 15 to 40 percent, and there is always a good selection.

The hours are: 10–9 M-F, 10–7 Sa, 11–6 Su. Major credit cards are accepted and all sales are final.

► HUFFMAN KOOS CLEARANCE CENTER
1800 LOWER ROAD, LINDEN, N.J.
(201-574-1212)

All week long the Huffman Koos stores all over New Jersey send their floor samples, returns, slightly damaged pieces, etc., to the clearance center, and on Friday, Saturday, and Sunday they are sold to the public at 30 to 60 percent below the store price. Since this is a very upscale furniture chain you may find extraordinary bargains here, but you may have to come more than once, to get what you want. Everything is sold "as is," so look it over carefully. It may be that the only flaw is the fabric or finish, which the original customer had not ordered—manufacturers do make mistakes.

Occasionally there are un-advertised special events at the outlet center—call to find out about them.

The hours are 12–5 F and Su, 10–5 Sa. Huffman Koos charge cards and major credit cards are accepted and all sales are final.

All the clearance centers mentioned above sell furniture from retail stores. When the showrooms that sell only to the design professions want to dispose of their samples and cancelled orders, they may send them to the:

▶ DECORATOR'S WAREHOUSE
616 WEST 46 STREET
(489-7575)

Five warehouse floors of furniture display manufacturers' overstock, showroom samples, cancelled orders, etc., from both decorator and better consumer resources. Some pieces are sold "as is," while others can be ordered in the finish and fabric of the customer's choice, because this is both a clearance center and a discount dealer for some brand-new furniture. Claimed discounts are 20 to 50 percent. Service is personal and salespeople are knowledgeable and helpful, never pushy.

The hours are 10–5 M–F, 11–5 Sa and Su. Credit cards are not accepted, but personal checks are welcome and all sales are final.

► O O P S
513 LA GUARDIA PLACE
(982-0586)

is a clearance center for a few high-style, mostly high-tech furniture manufacturers who usually sell exclusively to architects and interior designers. Only here is this furniture sold directly to the public, for at least 10 percent below the professional price. When design professionals buy furniture for their clients, they either mark it up for resale, or sell it for cost and charge a steep design fee, so buying at OOPS can really save you money in spite of the often very high prices. These pieces would cost much more elsewhere.

The hours are 12–6 Tu-Sa, 12–8 Th. Major credit cards are accepted and all sales are final.

DISCOUNT DEALERS

In addition to the outlets, there are furniture dealers who work from catalogues, keep their overhead low, and sell new furniture at discounts that are claimed to be as much as 40 percent. Usually, the higher the price, the greater the discount, but there are exceptions to this rule. A number of these dealers operate in Manhattan. The way to work with them is to shop the better stores, get the name of the manufacturer of a piece you like, the style number if possible, and, if you can, the identifying number for your choice of fabric. You can also work with pictures from magazines. Then go to the discount dealer and look at this manufacturer's catalogue. Find the pieces you are interested in and ask for a price quote and a delivery date. Is this fair to the retail store where you did your initial shopping? Not if you take up their salespeople's time without any chance of letting them make a sale. But if you just wander through their display like any other customer who is "just looking, thanks," you are really not doing any harm. Besides, there is always the chance that you will find something on sale, or fall in love with a piece that is exclusive with this store, and buy it.

Once you have chosen your furniture, you place your order with the discount dealer and wait for delivery, which can be directly from the factory or from a bonded furniture warehouse in your area. The warehouse should uncrate the furniture, inspect it to be sure it's in perfect condition, touch up the polish, deliver it to your home at a mutually convenient time (ask about Saturday delivery, if you need it), and place it where you want it.

A small piece, like a single chair or small table that is shipped in a carton, can be delivered directly from the factory to your door, but beware of sidewalk delivery of large pieces in crates. It's much cheaper than delivery through a warehouse, but it can result in all kinds of trouble.

Some discount dealers state in their literature that the shippers —not they—are responsible for adjustments, and that all complaints must be made to them. This is not as outrageous as it may sound, because furniture shippers who maintain a local warehouse are equipped to make minor repairs and authorized to return and replace unacceptable pieces. I still would not do business with a firm who works this way. You did not place your order with the shipping company, nor did you give them your payment. If there is a problem, the people who took your order and your money should be responsible, not the people who sent the truck.

There's only one respect in which the catalogue dealers may differ from a furniture store: they are often not factory-authorized, which means that they cannot buy directly from the factory, but must use a middleman. That is usually a dealer who is factory-authorized and who handles a large volume of orders for many of the catalogue dealers and order-takers with 800 telephone numbers. What you are buying from the catalogue dealer is gray market furniture. This explains why your dealer may not be able to handle your adjustments—he is not officially known at the factory.

Therefore, in addition to price and delivery date, ask the following questions: are you a factory-authorized dealer for this manufacturer? Will you charge me for shipping, and if so, how much? Shipping is expensive, so compare the discounted price plus shipping, with a price from an authorized dealer who may absorb the shipping cost. Then decide if the difference is worth the risk you take when you buy gray market goods. Consider also that the gray market dealer did not get the delivery date directly from the factory and cannot negotiate with them if the delivery is wrong or incomplete. City law protects you from missed delivery dates, but then you will still be without furniture and must start the waiting game all over.

Before making any major purchase, I would call the Better Business Bureau and find out if there are unresolved complaints against the dealer. If the dealer claims to be factory-authorized, I would also call the factory and confirm it.

I do not mean to draw an altogether grim picture—some gray market dealers have been in business for a long time and have satisfied customers. I only want to make sure that you also become a satisfied customer if you decide to buy furniture this way. If nothing goes wrong, you may save a lot of money, but things do go wrong, otherwise there would not be so much furniture in the clearance centers.

Currently the industry is in an uproar about gray market dealers who offer to ship furniture anywhere in the country. Understandably, the local dealers are not crazy about maintaining expensive real estate to be used as showrooms for other dealers whose overhead is lower. Model numbers and other information necessary for ordering are being disguised, and manufacturers are being pressured not to ship orders from authorized dealers to a location outside the dealer's delivery area. Several discount dealers in New York who flourished a year or two ago are now out of business.

The following dealers are well established and have large, if not very attractive, showrooms.

JAMES ROY
15 EAST 32 STREET (679-2565)

APARTMENT LIVING
12 EAST 21 STREET (260-5050)

▶ NEW YORK FURNITURE CENTER
41 EAST 31 STREET
(679-8866)

You can also order furniture from a store and still get a discount.

▶ ROMA FURNITURE
215 GRAND STREET
(925-8200)

I always look forward to seeing the windows of this store when I walk along Grand Street—they are so outlandishly pretentious, it's entertaining.

Recently I learned that in their upstairs showroom Roma also carries sleek, modern Italian imports—leather sofas and chairs, steel and glass tables, and lacquer pieces; Italian furniture is 85 percent of their business. On special order you can get some American and most imported lines, including high-style pieces that you may have seen in expensive specialty stores uptown. Their discounts are claimed to average 20 to 30 percent and are sometimes negotiable.

Roma has been in business for over fifty years. On my visit to the store I found everybody pleasant, helpful, and low-key—service with a big smile.

The hours are 10–9 M–Th, 10–6 F–Su. Major credit cards are accepted, and all sales are final.

Other Roma stores are located in Bensonhurst, Brooklyn, on Victory Boulevard, in Staten Island, and in Rockville Center, Long Island. Free parking is available at all locations.

▶ CARDARELLI FURNITURE
205 WEST HOUSTON STREET
(924-2040)

If you are looking for good traditional furniture from makers like Henredon, Century, Drexel Heritage, Hickory Chair, Kindel, and

Harden, look here. A complete home-furnishing resource, where you can also get carpeting, lamps, and lighting, this is a showcase store for some of the brands they carry. This means that they show the entire line—not just a few pieces—in their nine floor-through galleries. Service is pleasant and discounts are claimed to average 20 to 30 percent.

The hours are 9–5 M-Sa, 9–7 Th. Visa and MasterCard are accepted and all sales are final. Free parking is offered—call for directions.

▶ DESIGN FURNITURE WAREHOUSE
902 BROADWAY (AT 22ND STREET)
(673-8900)

The name is misleading, because this is a street-level retail store with room settings. The furniture comes from America, Europe, and Asia. Some is imported directly and priced very competitively. Other pieces, also carried by top department stores, are claimed to be 35 percent less here.

The hours are 10–6 M–F, 10–8 Th, 10–4:45 Sa, 12–5 Su. Visa and MasterCard are accepted and all sales are final.

▶ I K E A
1000 CENTER DRIVE, ELIZABETH, N.J.
(201-289-4488)

Shopping is a unique experience in this huge store, and the prices are fabulous. Ikea is a Swedish company with suppliers and stores all over the world, who are just beginning to saturate the American market. There are stores near Philadelphia, Baltimore, Washington, D.C., and Seattle. The Elizabeth store opened in May 1990, to be followed within a few months by stores in Burbank, California and on Long Island. Their buying power is tremendous, their standards of design and quality very high. Their designers are in Sweden, but furniture and furnishings are made exclusively for Ikea wherever the price is lowest and their standards can be met.

Start by ordering and browsing through their free catalogue. That will serve as your orientation for shopping in the store, where everything is attractively displayed in room settings, and you are given pencil and pad to write down your selections. Ikea has no salespeople, but red-coated aides wander through the store, ready to answer questions.

The furniture is Scandinavian in design and has simple, clean lines. There are lots of flexible storage pieces in various natural wood finishes and in white. Handsome leather sofas and sleep sofas are affordable here, and there is also dining and occasional furniture—one could easily furnish an entire home here. The practical, handsome office furniture is priced very reasonably. The storage pieces are sold "KD," in flat cartons, to be put together when you get home. Don't panic, it's part of the Ikea concept that anybody who can read an easy-to-follow instruction sheet can assemble the furniture. The few necessary tools are supplied in the package. I put together a chest of five drawers by myself, while watching two programs on TV. Not only was it easy to do, but the drawers fit precisely and ran more smoothly than factory-installed drawers in furniture twice the price.

When you have made your selection, you take it to a central desk, where prices will be added up. You will then be told where to pick up your purchases. Now the fun begins: everything is on giant steel shelves; you find it yourself, put it on a large supermarket-style cart, go to the check-out counter and pay for your furnishings as if they were chickens and oranges. You can have your purchases delivered, but you will save more if you take them home yourself. It's made very easy here: push your cart to a loading platform where a guard will watch it while you get your car. If a roof rack is needed, you can purchase it for a few dollars and return it for a full refund the next time you come to the store.

These unique merchandising techniques make it possible for Ikea to offer excellent quality at low prices. In addition to furniture, there are modular kitchen cabinets with innovative interior fittings,

Scandinavian-looking bathroom cabinets and commodes, colorful textiles, and a selection of lamps, tableware, cookware, and accessories.

You don't have to hire a babysitter to go shopping at Ikea. Strollers are parked near the entrance to the store, so babies can be wheeled along. Potty-trained toddlers check into the "Ball Room," a supervised space filled waist-high with plastic balls in which they wade, jump, and have a wonderful time. For older children there is a separate ball room and activities area with trained personnel, all courtesy of the management. There is also a big, bright self-service restaurant with Swedish food and reasonable prices.

Ikea is located in the Port Authority Industrial Park, near Exit 13A of the New Jersey Turnpike. N.J. Transit Bus #112 stops at the door on Saturday and Sunday. You can get the bus at the Port Authority Bus Terminal in Manhattan, or at the Elizabeth, New Jersey train station.

The hours are 11–9 M–F, 10–9 Sa, 11–6 Su. Visa and MasterCard are accepted and refunds given for any reason, indefinitely, as long as merchandise is returned in the original carton.

► OUTLET FOR DESIGN FURNITURE
500 NORDHOSS PLACE, ENGLEWOOD, N.J.
(201-567-0855)

These people have an interesting operation: they sell furniture from a limited group of upscale sources at a 30 percent discount, maintain their own showroom and warehouse, employ their own trained adjusters, and provide preliminary design services for a $300 fee. The design service can save you from making expensive mistakes: someone will come to your home in the greater New York tri-state area or in Florida, measure the rooms for which you require new furniture, and make a floor plan with suggested furniture layout and a color scheme for paint and upholstery colors.

When it comes to floor coverings and lighting you are on your own. They will make sure the furniture you select will fit comfortably into the room, can be brought up the stairs or the elevator, and will fit through the doorway. It's not the same as hiring your own interior designer, but it costs a lot less and takes care of the area that gives consumers the greatest headaches.

The furniture sold here is modern in style and of high quality: Emerson Leather, Classic Gallery, Tavola, Weiman, and Burton James are among the lines that are available. Everything is special order, nothing is in stock, but the store can sometimes reduce the waiting period.

The hours are 10–6 W–Sa. Visa and MasterCard are accepted and all sales are final.

FOAM FURNITURE

▶ DIXIE FOAM
611 AVENUE OF THE AMERICAS (AT 18TH ST.)
(645-8999)

If you have had inexpensive foam furniture and not liked it, don't conclude that all foam feels like jello; there is foam and there is foam, and the people at Dixie will explain the difference. Anybody with back trouble should seriously consider Dixie's top grade mattress, and anybody with a convertible sofabed should replace the very inferior mattress, when it wears out, with a good foam one— the difference is dramatic. Makers of convertible sofas may tell you that a foam mattress will not stand up to being folded during the day, but people who have tried it with top-quality mattresses from Dixie have had no problem. These mattresses are guaranteed for fifteen years. Besides beds you can get exercise mats and casual furniture. Foam can also be cut to order.

The hours are 10–6 M–Sa. Visa, MasterCard, and Discover cards are accepted here, and there is a 20 percent re-stocking charge on

refunds, which are given within ten days of purchase. There are no refunds on special orders.

SEE ALSO:

Economy Foam on the Orchard Street Walking Tour.

LUCITE AND PLEXIGLAS FURNITURE

▶ PLEXICRAFT
514 WEST 24 STREET
(924-3244)

Plexiglas and Lucite tables, serving carts, and other furniture is produced on the premises and sold directly to the public, without middlemen. This furniture is made of thick plastic with bevelled edges and has a quality look. Custom sizes are available and prices are claimed to be a minimum of 50 percent below retail.

Hours are 9:30–5 M–F, 11–4 Sa. Visa and MasterCard are accepted and store credit given within sixty days.

SEE ALSO:

ABC Carpet and Home in chapter 19.

LIGHTING

There is a section of the Bowery—between Grand Street and Delancey Street—where lighting stores are concentrated. They all sell lighting at good discounts, and yet they are not all alike. Merchandise and prices vary from store to store and it is best to comparison shop the whole area. Stores also occasionally get closeouts from manufacturers and slightly shopworn lamps are put on sale at prices that have been further reduced. If you are not up to shopping all the stores in the area you will do well at the following:

► PARIS INTERNATIONAL LIGHTING
164 BOWERY
(941-8887)

The store has been in this location for a long time, but it changed hands about a year ago. Now it is a very large lighting store that caters to all tastes and budgets. It sells many imports from Asia, where good lamps can be made for less than here or in Europe. Copies of expensive lamps from Italy sell for a fraction of the original price. I have seen those halogen desk lamps that are adjustable with the touch of a finger for $65 and $85, while the originals from Italy cost several hundred. The copies are well-balanced and function perfectly, and the manager assured me that if these delicate lamps ever went out of balance, he would adjust them free of charge. Halogen chandeliers, track lights, and other high-tech fixtures are available at similar prices.

There is a whole room full of crystal chandeliers, another with brass, and all manner of floor and table lamps, sconces, and lighting tracks. Prices are claimed to be a minimum of 20 percent below retail.

The hours are 8:30–6, seven days a week. Major credit cards are accepted and store credit given within seven days of purchase. Mail or phone orders are accepted for shipment via UPS.

▶ THRIFT HOUSE
185 BOWERY
(505-0300)

You will find few major brands here, but you *will* encounter a wide variety of imports from Italy and Taiwan which are well made, sold with a warranty, and very competitively priced. They are also producers of crystal chandeliers and Tiffany shades. If you bring a picture or explain an idea, they may be able to make a crystal chandelier in the size and design you specify. Many Tiffany shades are in stock. Your name or logo can be incorporated in the design of a shade, colors can be coordinated with those of your room, and sizes can be customized. Stained-glass panels for dropped ceilings, cabinet doors, room dividers, etc., are also available here. But they can be expensive.

Fringed silk lamp shades of stock materials cost $75–$150 when I looked, silk shades without fringes $60 and up. You can also bring in an old silk dress and have it made into shades, or use fabric from draperies or furniture in your home.

The store is open seven days a week: 10–5:30 M–F, 9–5:30 Sa, Su. Major credit cards are accepted and store credit given within two weeks of purchase, except on special orders.

▶ T H U N D E R A N D L I G H T
171 BOWERY
(219-0180)

The very modern, high-tech-looking halogen lighting here is manufactured in the company's own factory, and the owner claims that
this gives him the quality control that importers don't have. The
people here care not only about the aesthetics of the lamp, but
about the quality of the light you get in your home; they will even
make house calls. They also take care of installing track lighting,
which should be done by a specialist who knows just where to
place the track for best effect. The lamps come in a variety of
finishes and colors, and for large orders, custom colors are not out
of the question. Much of their business is custom work for architects and designers and prices are claimed to be 40 percent below
retail.

Open 8–6, seven days a week. Visa, MasterCard, and personal
checks are accepted and store credit given within fourteen days of
purchase, but all sales are final on special orders.

Not all lighting discounts are found on the Bowery; there is also:

▶ M A N H A T T A N L I G H T I N G
13 EAST 4 STREET
(254-6720)

This is a large, friendly store with a good selection of quality lamps
and ceiling fixtures, including halogens. They also carry halogen
bulbs and Hunter ceiling fans. Prices are claimed to be 20 to 40
percent below retail. The location is convenient—near off-Broad-
way theaters and restaurants, and across the street from Tower
Records.

The hours are 10–7 M–Sa, 11–7 Su. Major credit cards are accepted and store credit given within ten days of purchase.

Some of the best lighting bargains are found outside Manhattan.

▶ LAMP WAREHOUSE
1073 39 STREET, BROOKLYN
(718-436-2207)

This is claimed to be the largest lighting store in the country, but because they have expanded so often, it's actually a complex of stores now. Every type of lighting fixture from almost every manufacturer and importer, including halogen items and ceiling fans, is in stock, and sold at discounts that are claimed to be 10 to 40 percent.

This is also a good source for lampshades. Prices start at $12–$15 for a simple shade and go up to a lot more for handmade fabric shades with fringes. They do custom work on shades, will use your own fabrics if you wish, and will also repair, recover, and restore old shades. Most special orders can be filled in two weeks.

Mail and phone orders from anywhere can be filled, if the manufacturer's name and style number is supplied. You can also send a picture and consumer information from a magazine. The purchase will be charged to your credit card and shipped via UPS.

The warehouse is two blocks from the Smith and 9th Street station of the BMT subway line and street parking is usually available.

Discounts are claimed to be 20 to 50 percent, sometimes even more. *The hours are 10–5:30 M–F, 9–5:30 Sa–Su.* Major credit cards are accepted and store credit given within two weeks except on special orders; because so many people have supplied the wrong style numbers, the store now takes no returns on mail and phone orders. The trick is to send the information from the manufacturer's hang tag, not from the store's.

▶ CHANDELIER WAREHOUSE
40 WITHERS STREET, BROOKLYN
(718-388-6800)

This company is a producer of brass, crystal, and wrought-iron chandeliers; they have a showroom in Manhattan where only interior designers are admitted. In the warehouse, they sell to the public and perform some useful services as well: they can alter a design to fit your space and will deliver and install anywhere within a one-hundred-mile radius. In addition to their own products they sell lamps, wall sconces, and track lighting with either incandescent or halogen bulbs. Prices are claimed to be 10 to 15 percent below decorator's wholesale cost. Halogen lighting is claimed to be 50 percent below list price.

The store is in the Greenpoint section of Brooklyn and can be reached by subway. The nearest station is Metropolitan Avenue on the GG line.

The hours are 9–3 M–F. If they are open on Saturday, it's 9–4, but call to confirm it. Major credit cards are accepted and store credit given within thirty days.

A special store for lampshades:

▶ JUST SHADES
21 SPRING STREET
(966-2757)

Shades of every kind, in every imaginable material. Plain linen shades for modern interiors, custom shades made of your material, foil shades, parchment shades, silk shades, elaborate Victorian shades with braid trim, silk fringe—you name it, they make it. They suggest that you bring along the lamp, to be sure the shade will fit. There are so many sizes, one could get confused.

A big selection is in stock, but if what you need is not available, it will be custom made within two weeks. Prices are not the cheapest in town, but quality for quality, they compare favorably with custom shades at more expensive locations.

Open every day except Wednesday, 9:30–4. Credit cards are not accepted and all sales are final.

LIGHT BULBS:

▶ JUST BULBS
938 BROADWAY (AT 22ND ST.)
(228-7820)

carries every imaginable type of light bulb: if it is being made, you can buy it here. Prices are not discounted and they can be expensive, but you may not want to chase all over town for a good deal on a light bulb. This store offers convenience and selection.

Discounts on light bulbs are available, if you buy them in quantity at:

▶ WIEDENBACH-BROWN
435 HUDSON STREET
(243-4500)

This big wholesale distributor of light bulbs supplies retail chains, institutions, hotels, and office buildings with cases of light bulbs at wholesale prices. They will sell you anything you want if you come to Hudson Street, but it only gets interesting if you buy a case of 120. Count the fixtures in your house and divide 120 by that number; you will be surprised—in a few months you may use up a case, and you can save quite a bit. You can also buy packages of six, twelve, and twenty-four bulbs and still get 5 to 10 percent off. I learned that supermarkets mark lightbulbs up 50 to 60 percent, distributors only 10 to 20 percent. To my surprise the director of sales suggested that the customer negotiate the price, if he or she is not offered a good deal by the people in the showroom.

Wiedenbach-Brown sells everything made by G. E., Sylvania, and Ushio in almost every bulb you could need, including halogen, candle bulbs for chandeliers, tungsten, many kinds of fluorescents. Sometimes they get specials from G. E. and can offer even better bargains.

Open 8–5 M–F. Only cash is accepted and store credit is given within fourteen days of purchase.

HOME FABRICS

When you buy a piece of upholstered furniture, you usually select the fabric from a choice the manufacturer offers. You may then find that the advertised price goes up a lot, when you select a good fabric.

There is a better way: ask if the furniture can be bought C.O.M., which means customer's own material. Usually it is possible. You pay the basic price for the chair or sofa, but you don't get the basic fabric; you get your own fabric put on instead. Since it is harder for the workroom to use an unfamiliar fabric, the trade-off is fair. Of course the fabric you send has to be suitable for the piece, and some manufacturers may want to approve a sample cutting before accepting your order. If the salesperson from whom you buy the fabric knows his or her stuff, there should be no problem.

When you call in a firm to re-upholster, or to make slipcovers, fabric shades, or draperies, they too will bring fabric samples and if you select a good fabric, the price will be far higher than the minimum you were quoted originally. You never really know how much you are paying for labor and how much, by the yard, for fabric. Often it's the full retail price. In this case, too, there is a better way. Tell the upholsterer to quote you a price for labor only, and get better fabric for less money by shopping at one of the sources in this chapter. When you use inferior fabric you really don't save money in the long run.

The most durable fabrics on the market are produced for non-residential use and are rarely put on retail furniture. They are sold by the yard in showrooms that often don't deal with the public—only with architects and designers. These fabrics are sold from samples and it is important that the yardage that is shipped matches the sample closely. A bolt that does not match the sample automatically becomes a second, even though there may be absolutely nothing else wrong with it. It is often sold at a factory outlet or warehouse sale, and it is usually a great bargain. Check out the following outlets:

► S I L K   S U R P L U S
223 EAST 58 STREET (753-6511)

► S I L K   S U R P L U S
1147 MADISON AVENUE (794-9373)

► S I L K   S U R P L U S
449 OLD COUNTRY ROAD, WESTBURY, L.I. (516-994-7469)

► S I L K   S U R P L U S
281 MAMARONECK AVENUE, WHITE PLAINS (914-684-0041)

► S I L K   S U R P L U S
1210 NORTHERN BOULEVARD, MANHASSET, L.I. (516-627-3737)

Interior designers come here to find bargains for their clients, but these stores also sell to the public. These are the outlets for Scalamandre fabrics, the firm that furnishes authentic reproductions to historic preservations like Colonial Williamsburg. There are other imported and domestic fabrics here, some exclusive with Silk Surplus. There is also wallpaper, to match and coordinate with the fabrics, and an outstanding collection of tassels, braids, and other elegant trimmings.

Some of the offerings are seconds, sold "as is," but these are always clearly identified. It is then up to you to find the flaw and see if you can live with it.

Discounts are claimed to be 10 to 70 percent.

The hours are 10–5:30 M–F, 11–4 Sa. Visa and MasterCard are accepted, shipping is available, and all sales are final.

▶ I N T E R C O A S T A L   T E X T I L E S
480 BROADWAY
(925-9235)

Shopping here is not easy, but it's worth the effort. Two floors are piled to the ceiling with big bolts of fabric and your job is to find out what's on them and then visualize how it will look in your home. There are patient salespeople who will lift heavy bolts down from shelves and remove the ones that are "double parked" against the wall, so you can look at what's behind. If you want to see a color under different light (you probably should) or if you wonder how it will look with your rugs, buy a quarter yard and take it home—at these prices, you can afford it.

The price for these fabrics is often a small fraction of the original wholesale price; I have bought $60-a-yard upholstery fabric here for $5 and casement cloth for curtains for $2. Hardly anything, no matter how high the original price, is more than $15 a yard. How can they do it? They buy closeouts, overruns, discontinued patterns, leftovers from mills and converters; they pay cash and buy in very large quantities, because this is primarily a wholesale operation. Then they put a fair markup on their cost and voilà, phenomenal bargains. When I looked, Intercoastal carried prints from Marimekko, Riverdale, Schumacher, Covington, Kaufman, and Jay Yang; I also recognized woven upholstery fabrics from Jack

Lenor Larsen and Robert Allen, which usually sells for more than $100 a yard at retail.

Antique fabrics—over twenty-five years old—come in Art Deco and Victorian colors and patterns (depending on age) and may be better quality and more durable than what is being made today. On the other hand, you may hate the muddy period colors.

When you shop here, you may rub shoulders with scenic designers from stage and TV, a few adventurous decorators whose clients are on a tight budget, or housewives from Little Italy and women who work in nearby factories.

If you need the address of a good workroom for your upholstery or drapery needs, the owner is willing to make recommendations, but only if you buy your fabric here.

The hours are 10–6 M–Th, 10–5 F. Between October and Christmas they are also open Sundays, 10–4. Credit cards are not accepted, personal checks are welcome, and goods will be shipped when the check has cleared. If you want to take your fabric with you, come during banking hours so that your check can be verified—or pay cash. You can get store credit within seven days only if you buy an entire bolt. If your fabric is cut, it's final sale only.

WAREHOUSE SALES

The best, but hardly the most relaxed, way to get superb fabrics at affordable prices is at the occasional warehouse sales of fabric houses like Jack Lenor Larsen, Angelo Donghia, and China Seas. These sales are held from time to time when the warehouse needs cleaning out, and many people wait for them to get all the fabrics for their homes. Prices are fantastic—I once bought a bolt of $30-a-yard curtain fabric for $1 a yard—but there is utter confusion. You have to carry your own bolts to be measured and cut, have to wait a long time until it's done, and you will probably even wait a long time for the elevator. The atmosphere is tense and competitive, and you have to make instant decisions which you may regret later. You will, however, save a lot of money and get quality you would not dream of buying at full price, because these are very, very expensive fabrics. Sometimes there are also wall coverings. I know a woman who flew in from Pittsburgh, bought wallpaper and coordinating fabrics for her entire house, flew home that evening, and estimated that the trip saved her the price of an elegant vacation for two. Shipping via UPS is usually available and personal checks are usually accepted. There is no regular schedule for these sales, but they are often announced in the weekly city magazines. If you call the New York headquarters of the firms whose fabrics you admire, they may be able to tell you if and when a warehouse sale is planned.

▶ HARRY ZARIN'S WAREHOUSE
72 ALLEN STREET
(925-6134)

At this large operation where everything is in stock, you can either walk out with your yardage or have it sent the next day. This is unusual, because in many fabric stores you have to order from a sample and wait for delivery. What is even more unusual is the selection, which includes commercial grades as well as the most exclusive fabrics on the market. Clarence House, Schumacher, Robert Allen, and many similar mills are sold here, as well as upholstery Ultrasuede, French Tergal, and a big selection of the new tapestry fabrics. Prices are astounding: claimed discounts are always more than 50 percent, sometimes much more. There are some closeouts, but most of the stock is current, first-quality merchandise.

These big discounts are possible because everything is cut from bolts in stock that have been bought in quantity from the mill instead of from a middleman jobber. There is no special-order business and overhead is low.

A vast selection of curtain rods, hardware, hooks, tapes for draperies and Roman shades, can be found at Zarin's other store:

▶ B . Z . I .
105 ELDRIDGE STREET
(966-6690)

Here you will also find Venetian and vertical blinds by Levelor and Kirsch that can be made up in your size with a day's notice. They come in many colors and in macramé fabric as well, and prices are at least 50 percent below those at department stores. Laminated vertical blinds that can be made with your own fabric or wallpaper will take a little longer.

At both stores the hours are 9:30–5:30 Su–F. Major credit cards are accepted, shipping is available, and refunds are given within thirty days of purchase, but there is a 20 percent cutting charge for returning fabric that has been cut, none if you are returning the whole bolt. On special orders, the sale is final.

The firm has another store at 292 Grand Street, where hundreds of fabrics can be ordered from sample books. It is described on the Grand Street Walking Tour.

▶ B E C K E N S T E I N
118 ORCHARD STREET
(475-4887)

offers dress fabrics at street level and a large, comprehensive department for decorative fabrics on the second floor. Here there are no closeouts. Everything is current, first-quality merchandise, sold at substantial discounts. Fabrics by Waverly, P. Kaufman, Jay Yang, Kenmill, and others, are in stock, as well as imported tapestries and cotton velvet in 85 colors. You can order almost anything on the market from samples, including exclusive designer lines. See something in a magazine? Order it here at a discount.

Wallpaper by Imperial and Schumacher is available (you can order matching fabric), as well as window shades and blinds by Levelor, Delmore, and Hunter Douglas.

This firm believes in giving lots of individual service and attention. They maintain a sample matching service: send them a paint or carpet sample, or a sample of fabric you already have, and they will match it or suggest something complementary and send you a sample of it. Custom services include all sorts of window treatments, bedspreads, comforters, and upholstered headboards, pillows, slipcovers, and re-upholstery, but not from their own workroom; they send out the work

Twice a year, usually in February and July, there is a big remnant sale when three- to five-yard cuts of expensive fabric sell for $2 a yard. One remnant table remains in the store year round.

The hours are 9–5:30 Su–F. Major credit cards are accepted. Special-order items cannot be returned for credit, but anything from stock can be returned within thirty days, subject to a 25 percent cutting charge.

BED AND BATH

See the Grand Street Walking Tour. Also see ABC Linens in the following chapter on carpets and rugs.

CARPETS AND RUGS

Carpeting comes in big rolls and few dealers stock a large selection of it. The smaller the dealer, the less likely he is to have that sort of inventory, but he *will* show you hundreds of samples and he can, legitimately, get all these carpets for you. The difference is that the dealer pays a higher price for a "cut" (what's being cut off a big roll) and you will therefore pay more than when you select from the dealer's own inventory.

In the trade, anything that is cut from a roll is called carpeting; individual pieces are rugs or carpets. Of course, a piece of carpeting can be made into a rug, often by adding some sort of decorative border.

It is hard for a consumer to judge carpet quality. Fiber is no indication—it depends on how the nylon, polyester, etc., is produced, treated, made into yarn, dyed, woven or tufted, and finally backed. A shortcut during any of these steps can affect the quality of the final product. If you once had a nylon carpet that did not live up to your expectations, it is entirely possible that other nylon carpeting will perform better. Find a salesperson who does not insult your intelligence and tell him or her honestly what your priorities are. If you plan to move in two or three years, don't invest in carpeting that will last ten years. If you have small children or pets, the hard wearing "contract" qualities may be for you, but you will sacrifice softness. If you must have a particular color exactly, you will be very lucky to find it in stock—you may have to buy a cut. That's why it is good strategy to start your color scheme with the floor, while you can still be flexible. Stair carpeting must be of a quality that takes very hard wear, and a carpet in a studio apartment gets a lot more wear than one in a larger space. Having narrowed the choices this way, ask your reliable salesperson to show you samples from inventory and tell him or her that you know why these are the best value—you will command respect.

Carpeting is usually lined with a rubberized hair and jute backing which should be a 40 oz. weight, or a sponge backing which should weigh 50 oz. a square foot. The cost of the carpeting, plus the costs of lining and labor, delivery and tax, add up to what you pay, but the whole thing is quoted as one figure. The dealer's charges for lining of this quality and for labor vary between $9 and $13 a yard, or even more. If you want to know what you get for your money, ask what kind of lining the dealer proposes and how much lining and labor cost per square yard.

Carpet mills close out patterns that get old or do not sell well and they may offer a dealer the whole lot for a very cheap price, just to get it out of their warehouse. The carpet may be beautiful but a little too special for the mass market, and if it suits you, you get a great bargain. There are also trial rolls: when color lines are developed at the mill, a full roll of every proposed color is dyed, and if it does not look right, the formula is adjusted and it is dyed again. Then the merchandising people decide which colors to put in the line, and the most interesting ones often don't make it. These, too, are sold eventually by a discount dealer at a discount price.

One dealer with a big inventory of this kind is:

▶ MONTAUK CARPET
109 WEST 24 STREET
(691-2400) and
65 PRICE PARKWAY, FARMINGDALE, L.I.
(516-293-3900)

Montauk claims to be the largest carpet dealer on Long Island, and it has a vast inventory from many good mills at both its Manhattan and its Long Island locations. Their thick, nubby Berber textures are direct imports and very good value. Mill closeouts can often be sold to you for less than the wholesale price. The stores also carry carpeting with unusual patterns, borders, Victorian motifs, and decorative treatments, which all can be ordered. The budget figure for lining and laying here is $11 a yard.

Their rug collection, mostly 100 percent wool, includes custom designs made in Japan, imports from India, China, Belgium, Israel, Greece, Spain, and Portugal, in a wide range of designs, from Oriental to ultra-modern. Ceramic tile and vinyl flooring are also available here.

The Manhattan store is open 9–6 M–F, 10–3 Sa. In Farmingdale the hours are 8–9 M–F, 8–5 Sa, 12–9 Su. Credit cards are not accepted in either store and all sales are final, except for rugs, for which refunds are given within twenty-four hours.

▶ ABC CARPET AND HOME
888 BROADWAY and 881 BROADWAY (AT 19TH ST.)
(473-3000)

Here the claim is that ABC is the largest carpet store in the world; they have a vast inventory of mill closeouts, trials, and special purchases that often includes some very elegant carpeting. These can be seen in the store at 881 Broadway, across the street from the main store. In the basement of that building there are remnants —less than full rolls, but often enough for a single room or a small apartment. You should start your search there, where the prices are claimed to be 60 to 80 percent below prevailing retail prices.

Then check the inventory and if you don't find what you need there (which is unlikely), look at the vast selection of current production samples from which you can order. The budget figure for installation and lining, as specified above, was quoted at $10 a yard.

Across the street at 888 Broadway there is another vast inventory of rugs in natural fibers. On the first and second floor there are kilims, dhurries, Berbers, hooked rugs, what they call "Oriental Interpretations" which are machine-made, rag rugs, and sisal rugs. Custom rugs, in your choice of size and colors, can be ordered here as well.

On the fifth and sixth floors are the genuine, handmade Oriental, Chinese, needlepoint, Navaho, and tribal rugs from provenances that include the Far East, Iran, the Caucasus, Tibet, Russia, and the Navaho reservation.

The same building also houses antique furniture on the second and fourth floors. There is a large collection of armoires, imports from England, France, Scandinavia, India, and South America, as well as some quality reproductions of antiques that are in stock for immediate delivery. Both formal furniture and country antiques are featured.

There are no discounts in the bath and linen shop on the third floor. However, there are frequent sales and special promotions, and the private-label table linens are very good values. Sheets and towels are from Fieldcrest, Martex, Sheridan, and Des Champs, and there is a collection of bed and bath gift items like picture frames, mirrors, and boudoir pillows.

The hours are 10–8 M–Th, 10–7 Tu, W, F. 10–6 Sa, 11–5 Su.

The firm has another location:

▶ A B C   C A R P E T   W A R E H O U S E
1055 BRONX RIVER AVENUE, BRONX
(842-8770)

The company's inventory is too large to keep in one store so some is sold from the warehouse. Prices are comparable to those in the store, however, as this is not an outlet but an additional sales area. *It is open 7 days a week.* Call for hours and driving directions.

▶ RUG TOWER

399 LAFAYETTE STREET (AT 4TH ST.)
(677-2525)

A dramatic store in a landmark building that sells antique, semi-antique, and new one-of-a-kind handmade rugs at extremely competitive prices. The selection is enormous, and includes some very unusual pieces. There are Persian rugs from many provenances, kilims, needlepoint rugs, Indo-Persians and Tibetan rugs. No matter what your taste, decor, or budget, there will probably be something here you'll fall in love with and can afford; prices start at $70 and go up to the hundreds of thousands. The buyer has a very good eye for interesting designs and colors and a vast knowledge of his field—he used to be in charge of floor coverings for all Bloomingdale's stores, and that's just one of his impressive credits. There is state-of-the-art lighting so you can look at rugs under different lights and two station wagons on call to bring carpets to the setting for which they are intended, so you can see them in situ before deciding.

In the handmade rug business the dealer's integrity is very important, because few customers understand value. The staff here knows their carpets, like to share their knowledge, and will not tell you fairy tales.

The store is open seven days a week: 10:30–8 M–F, 10–6:30 Sa, 11–6 Su. Major credit cards are accepted and refunds given within seven days of purchase; this can be extended by mutual agreement if the purchase goes out of town. Rug Tower ships all over the world.

WALL COVERINGS

What's true about the furniture business is also true about wall coverings: if you know the name of the manufacturer and the style number, you can order wallpaper on the telephone from an out-of-town dealer and save a great deal of money. Unlike those in the furniture business, however, these are registered dealers who offer a huge inventory—there is nothing gray market about these transactions. The only way you will find names and numbers, however, is in another wallpaper store, where prices may be full retail. Naturally, the owners of these stores may not want their stores used as showrooms for discounters. To prevent this, they may disguise the sample books with coded style numbers of their own. Not many use this tactic, because it involves a lot of labor.

When you or your paperhanger decide on the number of rolls you need, it is a good idea to order a little more, because all the rolls should come from the same dye lot; otherwise the colors may not match exactly. Dealers usually let you return unused rolls, but many charge a re-stocking fee for returned merchandise.

Wallpaper is priced by the single roll, but sold only in double rolls, a confusing practice of which you should be aware.

▶ MARTIN SILVER
3001—5 KENSINGTON AVENUE, PHILADELPHIA, PA. 19134
(800-426-6600)

This is a large retail store that also does a big mail- and phone-order business, at claimed discounts of 40 to 66 percent. They carry almost everything that's on the market, from inexpensive mass-market papers to designer lines, from unusual silks, foils, and printed grasscloth to murals. If you cannot send them a style number, give them the name of the manufacturer, describe the design, and they will send you samples. Delivery is prompt, and when something is not immediately available they notify you at once. For returns and refunds, call within thirty days of receiving the goods and they will send shipping labels. When the shipment is received, they will issue a refund, but there is a 20 percent restocking charge.

Major credit cards are accepted.

SEE ALSO:

Sheila Wallstyles, on the Grand Street Tour, Beckenstein on the Orchard Street Tour, and Silk Surplus in chapter 18: Home Fabrics.

APPLIANCES

Since there are generally no suggested retail prices in the major-appliance business (it's every retailer for himself), the term "discount" is meaningless, but if you shop carefully, you should be able to save 15 to 25 percent off the price quoted by a conventional retail dealer.

It's not easy to shop intelligently, because every dealer shows different makes and models, and it's difficult to comparison-shop. However, *Consumer Reports* rates the best new models, reports on features, advantages, disadvantages, and prevailing prices. Find it in any library; it's a good way to start.

The manufacturer's local sales office may have a customer service department to answer questions and mail out brochures on request. General Electric answers all consumer questions at (800) 626-2000.

Once you have decided what you want, get price quotes from several dealers, and if the prices are essentially the same, deal with the one who is the most pleasant and patient.

► B E R N I E ' S
821 AVENUE OF THE AMERICAS (BETWEEN 28TH AND 29TH STREETS)
(564-8582)

For a TV or VCR, a refrigerator, or just a new curling iron or electric razor, this is a good place to shop. They sell all popular brands at prices that are claimed to be only 10 to 15 percent above wholesale.

There are food processors, electric irons, vacuum cleaners, small appliances, and personal-care items, as well as kitchen stoves, dishwashers, and all other major appliances.

The hours are 9–5:30 M–F, 11–3:30 Sa. Major credit cards are accepted and refunds given within seven days, if the item is in its original carton.

► J .   E I S   A N D   S O N
105 FIRST AVENUE
(475-2325)

This is an established neighborhood store for major appliances, but since the neighborhood is changing, Eis now caters to prosperous condo and loft owners. It's one of the few stores in Manhattan where you can see a selection of major appliances by General Electric, Whirlpool, Maytag, Welbilt, Sub Zero, and Friedrich on display, and be helped by a knowledgeable salesperson.

Open seven days a week 9–5:45 M–F, 9–2 Sa, 10–3:30 Su. Visa and MasterCard are accepted and all sales are final.

► U N C L E   S T E V E
343 CANAL STREET (226-4010)
216 WEST 72 STREET (874-3317)

This is a well-known discount dealer for audio and video equipment. The store on Canal Street is so busy that it can be hard to get attention, but selection is good and the price is right. In the store on Seventy-second Street there was only one other customer besides me one hot evening in July. The salesmen were huddled in a corner gossiping, but I still could not get anyone to help me.

They claim that they sell everything for 10 percent above cost, so prices here are good, even if service is not. The only form of payment accepted is cash and all sales are final. If there is something wrong with a purchase and you bring it back within seven days, they will replace it, but you cannot exchange it for anything else. After seven days you are on your own and must deal with the manufacturer directly.

The hours on Canal Street are 9:30–6:30 M–Sa, 11–5:30 Su. The Seventy-second Street store is also open late on Thursday evening.

There are several dealers of major appliances who take your order by phone if you know the brand and model number. The item is then delivered to you at an agreed-upon time (Saturday delivery is possible). You give the delivery person a check and receive the same warranty you would receive from a store, but you often get a better price.

► PRICE WATCHERS
(718-470-1620) OR (516-222-9100)

This dealer can get every major brand, including the very upscale ones. If you request it, they will make recommendations and discuss the relative merits of various models. If you prefer to make your own choice, they will get you exactly what you order, at prices that are claimed to be 15 to 25 percent below prevailing retail prices. There is a 2 to 4 percent charge for using a credit card, but personal checks are also accepted. Since everything is by special order, all sales are final. Saturday delivery is available.

► PENINSULA BUYING SERVICE
(838-1010)

The owner here is very knowledgeable and willing to make suggestions. He knows the very best refrigerators, cooking tops and ovens, audio components, TV sets and other appliances, which he often supplies for architect-designed homes, but if he thinks something is overpriced, he will tell you and suggest an alternative that is a better value. Of course he will also supply more prosaic needs. When I shopped for an apartment-size washer-dryer combination, he recommended one and when I asked if this was a really good unit, he said: "I will not lie to you, it's not the best, but it's adequate and it fits your space."

Prices are among the best, and exchanges or returns are possible. However, you pay for shipping it back, and that's expensive.

For more appliance dealers, walk on Canal Street from Allen to Essex Street and then turn left on Essex Street and walk to Grand Street. You will find many discount appliance dealers along the way. All have small stores, not much display, but large inventories are out of sight and many take special orders for major items. Major and small appliances, cameras, telephones, audio and video equipment, and everything else electric is discounted, so you can shop around until you find the best price or the nicest service. Most also carry popular appliances for 220 volt, which tourists from Europe and Israel pick up on their way to the airport, properly packed and invoiced. Come on a weekday, if you can—it's hectic on Sunday and of course every shop on the Lower East Side is closed Friday afternoon and Saturday.

SEE ALSO:

Century 21 and 47th Street Photo on the Lower Manhattan Walking Tour, Chapter 2; Kaufman Electronics and Grand Appliance and Giftware on the Grand Street Walking Tour, Chapter 4; Zabar's and Broadway Panhandler, in Chapter 22.

COOKWARE AND TABLEWARE

▶ Z A B A R ' S
2245 BROADWAY (AT 80TH ST.)
(787-2002)

On the street level is what Zabar's is famous for: an incredible
selection of gourmet food. Climb the stairs and find an equally
incredible selection of cookware and electric housewares at some
of the best prices in town. This is not "bargain" merchandise—it's
the finest money can buy, but here you need much less money.

This is not leisurely shopping, either. The aisles are narrow, the
place is always packed, and help is hard to get. But never mind,
the selection is enormous, the prices are low, and the savings are
worth the inconvenience.

Toasters, coffee makers, blenders and food processors, vacuum
cleaners, steam irons, automatic rice cookers, electric woks, and
anything else electric is available in a wide selection of models and
colors. There is a whole wall full of copper cookware lined with
stainless steel, the heavy kind that is pricey but a joy to use.
Cuisinart stainless steel commercial cookware is 30 percent off
retail, Henkel knives are heavily discounted, and a little gadget
called Micro Seal allows you to fill your own boil-in bags with

homemade food. Heavy, plain white tableware from China is handsome and very inexpensive: a cup and saucer was $1.98 when I looked, a large dinner plate $2.69. Large copper mixing bowls were $11.98, but one had a little dent, so it was reduced to $6.95; I have seen similar ones elsewhere for $30.

The hours are 9–6 seven days a week and major credit cards are accepted. Refunds are given within fourteen days of purchase.

▶ BROADWAY PANHANDLER
520 BROADWAY (BETWEEN SPRING AND PRINCE STREETS)
(966-3434)

Not as hectic or crowded as Zabar's, on some items perhaps not as cheap, this store offers an excellent selection of cookware, but no vacuum cleaners, electric irons, and other housewares items. It's a good resource for serious cooks and bakers and a pleasant place to shop.

The Panhandler's prices on Calphalon pots are 20 percent below retail, and so are prices on Master Chef—heavy aluminum with a stainless steel lining that gives you the advantages of both and none of the disadvantages. Le Creuset, the enamelled cookware from France, is expensive, but here the discounts are almost 40 percent. There is a handsome line of copper cookware from Brazil here, lined with stainless steel and more affordable than the French imports. They claim the biggest selections of bakeware in the city, including all the European sizes. Knives are by Wusthof and Suchi, a Japanese brand not yet well known here, which offers good quality at a gentle price. Small appliances, food processors, and a lot of useful gadgets are also available.

The hours are 10:30–6 M–F, 11–5:30 Sa. Major credit cards are accepted and store credit given within seven days of purchase. Shipping is via UPS. Mail or phone orders can be filled.

► LOUIS KAPLAN RESTAURANT
EQUIPMENT
250 LAFAYETTE STREET (BETWEEN PRINCE AND SPRING
STREETS)
(431-7300)

Come here for a dozen glasses, a set of stainless-steel flatware, a set
of dishes, or to have your whole kitchen re-designed and
equipped.

This firm has been outfitting hotels, restaurants, and clubs with
the best, and recently they have opened their doors to the general
public. Some of their tableware is exceptionally nice, and you will
not believe the prices—they are always wholesale. Minimum
quantity on most items is just one dozen, and the selection is
enormous.

There is, for instance, white dinnerware from France, made of a
material similar to Corningware, unbreakable and ovenproof. You
may not want to serve a formal dinner on it, but it's good-looking
for casual use and costs about half the retail price of Corningware.
The most elegant tableware I saw was the restaurant-quality Lenox
porcelain. Too expensive for most restaurants, it is popular for
executive dining rooms and private clubs. The quality is as fine as
the Lenox china for home consumption, but it is made to take
rough handling without breakage, in spite of the delicate appearance. Even at wholesale it's expensive, but the open-stock policy is
an advantage. No minimum quantity, no sets; just order what you
want, even one piece at a time.

Kaplan imports flatware directly, and there are handsome patterns available, in both stainless steel and silverplate. Restaurant
flatware is much stronger than the consumer quality. Try, hard, to
bend it out of shape—you will not succeed. One handsome stainless steel set looked so much like silver that even general manager
Tony Monier was confused for a moment. When I looked, I priced
a dozen each of dinner forks, salad forks, soup spoons, knives, and
teaspoons and the total was $82; and that's not even their cheapest
quality.

Practical resturant glasses have to be bought in full cartons of three dozen, but for crystal the minimum is usually one dozen. How can you tell the difference? Flick the edge with your fingernail: if you hear a bell-like ring, it's crystal. Glass of every conceivable size, shape, and quality is on display: Coke glasses, brandy snifters, glass mugs, and fluted champagne glasses, as well as glass pitchers, dessert dishes, salad servers, and dinnerware.

Copper, stainless steel, and heavy aluminum pots and pans are good buys, but many are too large for household use. We did see a heavy aluminum saucepan in 2¾-quart size with a silverstone lining for $10, and an 8" omelette pan for $12.

Chefs always work with their own set of knives, and they buy the best, but not necessarily a familiar brand. You can get top quality here for about half the price of Sabatier or Henkel.

The sleek modular stainless steel wire shelving that you have seen in photographs of high tech kitchens can be made up to fit any space exactly or made into serving carts with butcher block tops; either way, it will cost less than half the uptown retail price. Oven and cooking thermometers, stainless-steel ladles and cooking spoons, wire whisks, skimmers, and all sorts of useful gadgets come in sturdy commercial quality and will give better service than what consumers are used to.

If a new kitchen is in your future, check out the appliances here before you finalize your plans; they offer features like refrigerated drawers and custom sizing which may not be available elsewhere.

The hours are 9–5 M–F. Personal checks are accepted, but credit cards are not. Store credit is given within thirty days of purchase, but on special orders there is a 25 percent re-stocking charge.

▶ L A N A C   S A L E S
73 CANAL STREET
(226-8925) OR (800-522-0047)

A class act on Canal Street, Lanac stocks dinnerware from Lenox, Royal Doulton, Haviland, Pickard, Spode, Mikasa, Villeroy and

Boch, Bernardeau, and many others. Crystal glassware comes from Orrefors, Baccarat, Lenox, and Gorham; flatware in both silver and stainless steel is from Wallace, Reed and Barton, Kirk Stiffel, International, Lunt, Jensen, Retroneu, and Yamasaki. Anything not in stock can be ordered, but waiting time may be as long as twelve weeks.

Discounts vary from 20 to 45 percent. Prices are quoted over the telephone and shipping via UPS is available; there is also a bridal registry.

The hours are 10–5 Su, 10–6 M–Th, 10–2 F. Visa, MasterCard, and Discover are accepted and store credit given within fourteen days of purchase, but on special orders all sales are final.

You don't have to go downtown for upscale tableware bargains. In the chic high-rent area, you will find the amazing

▶ ROBIN IMPORTS
510 MADISON AVENUE (54TH STREET)
(753-6475) OR (800-223-3373)

This is a small store with an enormous stock of porcelain and stoneware, stainless steel and silverplate, table linen, barware, stemware, candlesticks, serving pieces, and accessories. A partial listing of brands includes Arabia, Fitz and Floyd, Gorham, Meissen, Rosenthal, Royal Limoges, Spode, Wedgewood, Villeroy & Boch, Dansk, Retroneau, Towle, Lalique, Val St. Lambert, Crystal Sevres, Orrefors, and a great deal more; send for their complete listing. Discounts are claimed to be 20 to 40 percent. What's not in stock can be ordered for delivery in two to three weeks.

Table linens include embroidered imports from Ireland and Asia, as well as wash and wear tablecloths and place mats, in prints and solids, from domestic manufacturers. Discounts on linens are claimed to be 30 to 40 percent. Robin ships all over the world.

The hours are 9:30–5:30 M–F, 10–5 Sa. Major credit cards are accepted and store credit given within thirty days.

▶ JEAN'S SILVERSMITH
16 WEST 45 STREET
(575-0723)

Here you will find a large stock of estate silver, antique jewelry, and discontinued flatware patterns, so you can replace those missing teaspoons. Current flatware and holloware can be ordered here for a claimed discount of 30 to 40 percent. When a manufacturer has a special promotion, the discounts can be even better.

9–5 M–Th, 9–4 F. Visa and MasterCard are accepted and store credit is given within fifteen days on everything but special orders.

▶ MICHAEL C. FINA
580 FIFTH AVENUE
(869-5050)

A large store with a comprehensive display of porcelain and pottery table settings, silver and stainless steel flatware, and crystal glassware; whatever you have seen in a full-price retail store can probably be found here for 20 to 50 percent less. They issue an elaborate catalogue and do a big phone and mail order business.

The hours are 9:30–6 M–F, 10:30–6 Sa, open to 7 Th. Major credit cards are accepted and refunds given within three months.

Outside Manhattan—and worth the trip—is the:

▶ MIKASA WAREHOUSE
25 ENTERPRISE AVENUE NORTH, SECAUCUS, N.J.
(201-867-2324)

This is actually an enormous store, where all of the firm's tableware, glassware, flatware, cookware, and accessories are sold at claimed discounts of 40 percent. Only a few patterns that are restricted to certain stores don't make it here, and you will find a big selection in this bright place where you shop supermarket style, with a shopping cart. People at the information desk are patient and helpful, so you are not on your own—your questions will be answered by experts. If you want your bargains shipped, you can arrange for it at the check-out counter.

During two mammoth sales in December and around Mother's Day, things are priced even lower and people come from far and wide for the super bargains. It's very crowded, and you may have to stand in line to even get into the store. If you find this sort of shopping a bit traumatic and you are happy with a big selection and 40 percent discounts, come when it's calmer.

Open seven days a week 10–6 M–W and Sa, 10–9 Th, F, 12–5 Su. Visa and MasterCard are accepted and store credit given within ten days. This credit must be used within a year of the day it is issued.

▶ DANSK FACTORY OUTLET
WOODBURY COMMON, CENTRAL VALLEY
(914-928-9903)

Distinctive enamel casseroles, teak carving boards, dinnerware, and table accessories from Dansk are discounted here up to a claimed 60 percent, but when I looked, nothing seemed cheap. Selection was very comprehensive and I suspect that the discontinued patterns and seconds which they advertise are augmented with regular merchandise at smaller discounts.

10–6 M-Sa, 11–5 Su. Visa and MasterCard are accepted and all sales are final.

There is another Dansk store in Flemington, New Jersey.

SEE ALSO:

East Side Gifts, Goldman on the Grand Street tour; and Pearl River Emporium, Wing on Wo on the Chinatown tour.

FLOWERS AND
PLANTS

If your early memories include walks in the countryside and coming home with an armful of flowers, or buying them for pennies at farm stands along the road, you probably feel deprived. Even if you buy fresh flowers only for special occasions, it hurts to pay current prices. I don't know any stands in the city at which pennies will buy even a single bloom, but farmers' markets and supermarkets often have bargain plants, and there are other good alternatives to floral destitution.

▶ ROSA ROSA
831A LEXINGTON AVENUE (AT 63RD ST.)
(935-4706)

Only roses are sold here and they sell a lot of them, so they can keep prices low. The small, short stemmed variety is usually $5 a dozen, larger roses with longer stems are $7. These are not puny leftovers but full blooms with good color which keep a long time, because they are very fresh when they are sold. Available colors are usually pink, red, yellow, and off-white. The store makes no deliveries and flowers are sold plain, but if you want baby's breath, it's available for $2 a bunch. They also sell vases.

The hours are 9–8 M–Sa, 5–7 Su. American Express is accepted.

Rosa Rosa was the first of its kind, but now red bargain roses are cropping up all over town. Perhaps there is one in your own neighborhood. Remember, however, the fresher the roses, the longer they last. If you bought some that did not last, try another store the next time. Street vendors seldom have fresh flowers, but supermarkets sometimes do.

▶ UNIVERSITY GOURMET AND FLOWERS
116 UNIVERSITY PLACE
(243-3139)

This is a simple flower stand outside a gourmet shop, under the separate management of "Lee," a gentleman who knows his flowers. Last winter he had carnations for $3.99 a dozen, purple pom poms, large daisy pom poms or blue irises for $2.99 a bunch and roses for $5.99, $6.99, $7.99, and $8.99, depending on length of stem and size of bloom. If you spend $25 here he will deliver anywhere in Manhattan for a $5 charge.

The store is open twenty-four hours, seven days a week and accepts no credit cards.

The wholesale district for flowers and plants, where florists shop, is located around 6th Avenue, between Twenty-fifth and Twenty-eighth streets. The true wholesalers will sell to anybody with a resale tax number, but other consumers cannot shop there because they don't want to be burdened with the clerical chore of collecting sales tax.

There are a number of good retail shops right here in the wholesale area, where prices are far below those of the average neighborhood store and the flowers are always fresh. Some stores have a big inventory of plants and indoor trees, others have outstanding selections of dried flowers, grasses and silk flowers.

▶ BILL'S FLOWER MARKET
816 SIXTH AVENUE
(889-8154)

There are not only silk flowers here, but also interesting silk vegetables and dried flowers and grasses. Cut flowers and arrangements are well-priced, and service is reliable.

The hours are 7:30–4 M-Sa, and major credit cards are accepted.

▶ HOLLAND PARADISE
800 SIXTH AVENUE
(684-3397)

The sidewalk display here has the prettiest flowering plants in the neighborhood and the basement the best silk flowers and silk trees. On the street floor there are lush hanging baskets, pots of orchids, indoor trees, and cut flowers. The three spirited owners, Mesdames Lina, Maria, and Marta keep busy making bouquets and arrangements. They use fresh, dried, and silk flowers—or a combination of all three—and they are prepared to design arrangements for every occasion. Their clientele includes celebrities from the worlds of fashion, show business, television, and politics, who like a quality bargain as well as the rest of us. Prices are claimed to be 30 to 50 percent below neighborhood retailers and way below society florists on the Upper East Side. Other services here include interior landscaping and maintenance.

The hours are 9–6, seven days a week. Visa and MasterCard are accepted.

▶ PEOPLE'S FLOWERS
786 SIXTH AVENUE
(686-6291)

Very large decorative cacti were on display here for $45 and $65 the day I visited. Because they require so little care, these plants would probably thrive in a New York apartment. I also saw cherry blossom and dogwood branches for forcing, and evergreen garlands that had been flame retarded, but ignore the silk flowers here: they were reminiscent of a cheap hat shop at Easter time, circa 1950.

The hours are 8:30–5:30 M–Sa, and major credit cards are accepted.

▶ P A R K   P L A N T S
774 SIXTH AVENUE (AT 26TH STREET)
(696-9830)

Dried flowers, cacti—including the large dramatic ones—and exotic plants are what you find here in profusion. Prices are excellent. Twice a year, for Christmas and Easter blooming, they have great amaryllis plants for $6.00 each—an outstanding bargain.

Open seven days a week, 8–6. Major credit cards are accepted and all sales are final.

FOOD

You want to entertain elegantly and eat well even when you are alone, but you don't want food to wreck your budget. It's a challenge, but with the right addresses and a little organization, it can be done. You will have to plan ahead and make time for some shopping in shops far from home. The best strategy is for two people to go in a car once a month, and hit all the epicurean bargain sources. This allows one to shop while the other holds the fort. There is also no limit to what you can carry, and you can get around faster. When you get home, cook ahead, stock the freezer, and the rest of the month just pop home-cooked meals in the microwave.

Where to shop:

MEAT

▶ OLD BOHEMIAN MEAT
452 WEST 13 STREET
(989-2870)

A wholesaler and restaurant supplier who will sell to you too, if you take their minimum quantities, which are manageable:

Flank steak, 2½–3 lbs minimum at $3.75 per lb
Rack of lamb, 6–8 lbs minimum at $3.60 per lb
Chopped meat, 3–5 lbs minimum at $1.70–$2.50 per lb
Loin of pork, 9–12 lbs minimum at $1.75 per lb
Leg of lamb, 9–12 lbs minimum at $1.85 per lb
Veal cutlets, 5 lbs minimum at $7.95 per lb
Veal roast, 5–8 lbs minimum at $3.90 per lb
Filet Mignon, 7–9 lbs minimum (trimmed) at $4.75 per lb

Other cuts have larger minimums, but everything will be cut and wrapped to your specifications, ready for the freezer. They also have whole chickens, chicken breasts, and chicken cutlets, Cornish hens, ducks, capons, rabbits, venison, and all sorts of sausages and cold cuts.

You can place your order by telephone, but must pick it up by 2:30. Only cash is accepted, and quality is excellent.

The hours are 6–3:30 M, Tu; 6–4:30 W; 6–6 Th, F.

▶ BASIOR SCHWARTZ
421 WEST 14 STREET
(929-5368)

The meat here is very good and reasonable, as are a great many other items, including excellent cheeses, good frozen cakes, pâtés from Trois Petites Cochons, smoked salmon from Nova Scotia, sun-dried tomatoes, olives, cornichons, cepes and porcini mushrooms vacuum-packed in one-pound cans, Dijon mustard, bakery style cookies in one-, two-and-a-half-, and five-pound packages, wild rice, and deli-style cold cuts (ham, roast beef, turkey breast) in three- to ten-pound pieces, unsliced. There are also very fresh eggs and wonderful sweet butter, whole filets of beef and boneless shells which you must cut yourself, sirloin tips in ten-pound bags for $25, for Boeuf Bourgignon or classy stews. Prices are truly wholesale, but you must take minimum quantities.

If you are a night person or a very early riser, it helps—the hours are geared to the needs of the wholesale trade: 5–10 AM. Cash only.

▶ K U R O W Y C K Y
124 FIRST AVENUE (BETWEEN 7TH AND 8TH STREETS)
(477-0344)

This shop has beautiful kielbasa sausages, cooked meat loaves and veal loaves, superior frankfurters, all kinds of hams and European cold cuts, and a great deal more. Try the dried Polish mushrooms (for mushroom barley soup and for stews), their honey, preserves, and—in the summer—raspberry syrup to be mixed with seltzer for an aromatic soft drink. Take home some Lithuanian rye bread. Quality is superb and the prices will be a pleasant surprise.

The hours are: M–Sa, early morning till 6 PM. Cash only.

Getting a bargain on *fresh fish* is a little harder, but you often can at the:

▶ G R E E N M A R K E T   O N
U N I O N   S Q U A R E

Open Wednesday, Friday, and Saturday from 8 AM until the vendors are sold out, which can be quite early.

The Greenmarket, which is a real farmers' market, is great for local fruits and vegetables with a lot of flavor, vine-ripened tomatoes, hydroponically grown year round, fresh herbs, smoked meat, free range chickens, raw honey and baked goods; try a loaf from "Bread Alone." Their truck is there only on Wednesday and Friday and sells out early. Munch the bread, and you'll know why.

Several Long Island fishermen come here with their catch and prices are reasonable, if not cheap.

This is the biggest and most gourmet of the city's farmers' markets, but not the only one. Call GREENMARKETS 566-0990 for locations and days of other farmers' markets.

FRESH PASTA

There is really nothing easier on an evening when you don't want to cook—boil some fresh pasta, warm up some sauce or just sprinkle it with olive oil and cheese, and dress some salad greens; the whole thing takes less than ten minutes and is a lot more satisfying than fast food. The trick is to have the pasta and sauce on hand in the freezer.

▶ RAFETTO
144 WEST HOUSTON STREET
(777-1261)

is a wholesale supplier of good restaurants which is also popular with retail customers from Soho and Greenwich Village. Their pasta is made daily and can be cooked within three days or frozen for future consumption.

There are meat, cheese, spinach, mushroom, and seafood ravioli, gnocchi, meat and cheese tortellini, noodles of every size from angel hair to very wide. They come white, whole wheat, or flavored with spinach, tomato, saffron, black pepper, or squid ink, which makes exotic-looking black noodles. Minimum quantity is 1 pound.

Sauces by Papa Lomagi are sold fresh here in 14-ounce containers. The selection includes marinara, puttanesca, primavera, meat sauce, pesto, and several other flavors. There is also parmigiano reggiano, romano, and provolone cheese, olive oil, canned tomatoes from Italy, and a vast selection of dried pasta shapes.

Prices are very reasonable—just a little above wholesale.

▶ BRUNO RAVIOLI CO.
653 NINTH AVENUE (BETWEEN 45 AND 46 STREETS)
(246-8456)

The original Bruno, who started this business in 1888, introduced ravioli to the U.S. and made it a commercial product for the restaurant trade. His granddaughter's husband runs it today. Now they also have a retail shop, where a staggering variety of fresh pasta is sold: ravioli and manicotti filled with meat, cheese, spinach and cheese, broccoli and cheese, sun-dried tomato and cheese, pesto and cheese, spinach, carrots and mushrooms, shiitake mushrooms, or seafood (a crabmeat, shrimp, and lobster mixture). Tortellini are stuffed with porcini mushrooms, capeletti with Gorgonzola, and angelatti with pesto. There is ready-to-heat lasagna filled with meat and cheese or vegetables and cheese, as well as Tortelloni stuffed with pumpkin or cheese. Pesto sauce, gourmet tomato sauce, and Alfredo sauce are made on the premises and sold in containers, ready to heat. Fettucini, linguini, and taglianini noodles come white, spinach-, or beet-flavored and look wonderful mixed in a tri-color dish.

Parmigiano and romano cheeses come grated and packaged; ricotta and fresh mozzarella come from an old-fashioned farm in New Jersey, where it is made in small batches. A good French bread from the Policastro bakery in Hoboken is available fresh daily. Prices are reasonable and quality is high.

The hours are 7–5:30, M–F, 8–5 Sa.

SEE ALSO:

Piemonte Ravioli and Di Palo's Latticini on the Grand Street tour.

HORS D'OEUVRES

▶ HORS D'OEUVRES UNLIMITED
4209 DELL AVENUE, NORTH BERGEN, N.J. 07047
(212-289-6667) OR (201-865-4545)

These hot or cold tidbits are passed at cocktail time in the best hotels, at diplomatic receptions and in elegant homes. They are sold flash frozen, usually in boxes of 100, to be cooked in the oven for fifteen minutes and served hot. There are also attractive cold canape trays, very useful for office parties. It's nice to keep a small assortment in the freezer and warm up a few when people drop in.

There are 120 varieties of hors d'oeuvres here, including cold canape trays, stuffed mushrooms, crabmeat or shrimp puffs, miniature pizzas or quiches, cheese or anchovy straws, empanadas, clams casino, beef kebabs, and a lot of other delicious things, priced from below $20 up to $54 for 100 bacon wrapped scallops. Most offerings are between $20 and $30. There are also many vegetarian dishes and kosher ones are available.

The bad news is that orders for less than $100 have to be picked up, while larger orders can be delivered for a fee. Call or write for a complete menu and price list that also contains useful hints on how many to buy for an event and instructions on how to get there. Since volume is big, everything is always in stock and always rotated: you will never get a dehydrated or freezer burned package as you might in a supermarket.

The hours are 7:30–3:30 M–F and some Saturdays in November and December from 9–2, but call to be sure.

▶ ROCCO PASTRIES
243 BLEEKER STREET
(242-6031)

You can order cakes of all sizes, round or rectangular, in white or chocolate dough, frosted with any color buttercream and decorated to suit the occasion. Order it a day in advance and pick it up when you want it; it will be impeccably fresh, not too sweet, and delicious. Prices are very reasonable. Delivery is not available.

Open 7 days a week, 7 am to midnight. Cash only.

▶ T O P   T O M A T O
670 BROADWAY (BLEEKER STREET)
(228-0080)

This is the twelfth store of a chain but the first in Manhattan, and when I visited soon after the opening, they were still getting to know their customers' tastes. On a cold day in January there was green asparagus for $1.99 per pound, white asparagus for $2.99, endive for $1.99, snow peas for $1.99, red or yellow peppers for $0.99, fresh mushrooms for $1.99. For $8.99 there were five varieties of exotic wild mushrooms, and there were fresh herbs in profusion. Also available were football-size pink grapefruits, kiwis, and stem strawberries. I didn't see any imported, vine-ripened tomatoes, which are expensive winter staples in many homes, and I would have preferred the bananas for $0.25 a pound a little riper.

The fish on mountains of ice is worth a trip from another part of town, and the counter was mobbed with customers who wanted fresh sardines from Portugal for under $3.00 per pound, super-jumbo shrimp for $5.95, and salmon, fresh tuna, mackerel, flounder filets, scallops, snapper, and many exotic varieties, at similar discount prices. Everything was fresh and beautifully presented. There was not a whiff of fish odor.

A salad bar ($2.99 a pound) included seafood salads, and two kinds of homemade soup—like minestrone, split pea, or clam chowder—are available every day for $1.50 a cup. The bakery counter offered small loaves of good Italian bread for $0.50, all sorts of muffins, croissants, bagels and rolls, very rich cakes, and cannoli for only $0.60.

Coffee is served in the bakeshop and there are tables and chairs up a circular staircase, where one can eat purchases on the spot. There is also a juice bar, a fresh flower stand, and a newsstand. *Open 7 days a week, 8–9.* Cash only.

SEE ALSO:

Russ and Daughters, Economy Candy Store, and Yonah Schimmel
on the Orchard Street Walking Tour; May May Food Co. and Maria
on the Chinatown Tour, and Cheese of All Nations on the Lower
Manhattan Walking Tour.

BEAUTY AND HEALTH

FREE HAIR COLOR AND PERMANENT WAVES

A great deal of research and testing goes into the products that are used to color your hair. In the final stages of development, these products are tested on live hair, not once but through several re-touches, to see how it wears and how stable the color is, as well as to check a lot of nuances on different textures and original hair colors. They do the same thing when the formula on an existing shade is adjusted and improved. Since there are dozens of products with dozens of shades each, these companies can use a lot of test models and you can be one of them, if they are working on your color. Some also do permanent waves, streaking, and highlighting.

▶ L'ORÉAL
575 FIFTH AVENUE
(818-1500)

For the service described above, call and ask for the Technical Center. If you become a test model, you will be asked to come for regular monthly color appointments, when your hair will be colored, conditioned, and set or blown dry. You can also have permanent waves here. If you do, you will be asked to come back a few times to have your hair washed and groomed, so the wave can be observed.

The L'Oréal Professional Beauty Institute gives training classes to hairdressers. People at the top of their profession teach the newest styles and techniques and students work on live models. If you are interested in being one of these models, call the above number and ask for the L'Oréal Institute.

Both facilities accept women and men for their services. The salons are extremely pleasant, the hairdressers are experienced, and the whole thing is completely free, except for the tip you will want to give your operator.

▶ CLAIROL ,EVALUATION CENTER
345 PARK AVENUE
(546-2715)

The object here is to evaluate Clairol products over a period of time, so you join a program and then come for monthly appointments. First you must have an interview any Monday, Wednesday, or Thursday from 9:30–11:30 or from 1:30–4. Your needs for hair color, hair care, permanent waves, highlights, relaxers, or Charlie Curls will be discussed and you will be told when a program to suit you is planned. What is expected from you is a commitment to keep these monthly appointments. No appointment is needed for the interview, and all services are free of charge.

▶ CLAIROL CONSUMER'S FORUM
345 PARK AVENUE
(546-2702)

Here you test Clairol products and tell them what you think of them. It's part of their ongoing product research and takes place on the first floor, 11–2 M–F, by appointment. You may be testing an appliance or a hair care or skin care product and you may come three times a year.

At the end of a program in either facility you will get a gift of a Clairol appliance or Clairol products.

► **JINGLES INTERNATIONAL ADVANCED HAIR TRAINING CENTER**
350 FIFTH AVENUE
(695-9365)

In the sub-basement of the Empire State Building is a school where successful hairdressers and salon owners pay good money to learn the latest techniques and styles. New classes start every week and every student needs a good head of hair to work on.

You must be willing to let your hairdresser cut your hair an inch or two shorter than the length you walk in with, and you may be in the hands of talent—or not—but in any event a teacher, who is a very good hairdresser, will supervise.

Where do hairdressers learn to be good enough to work in top New York salons? Right in the salon. Many have their own training programs and you can be one of the "models." It's either free or very inexpensive, but there is a tradeoff: you must let them give you a new style, which may or may not delight you. You must also be prepared to have your hair cut shorter, except if they are working on braids and chignons. After all, you are lending your hair for a creative effort and you must let your hairdresser create, although you will always be consulted. Your lifestyle and taste will be considered—at least in theory.

Good-looking people with good hair have done very well at these sessions. One woman who went to Sassoon a few years ago was invited to have her hair done free for six months and was then occasionally flown to conventions and shows on weekends to model Sassoon styles and go to all the parties.

To become a styling model, you usually show up at a specified time, get looked over as to your suitability for the evening's lesson, and either chosen as a model or sent away ungroomed. It depends on how many people show up and if someone wants to work on your particular hair. Schedules for training sessions vary, so call the following salons and ask when they are held:

Nardi, 143 E. 57 Street (421-4810)
David Daines, 833 Madison Avenue (535-1563)
Vidal Sassoon, 767 Fifth Avenue (535-9200)
Bruno le Salon, 16 West 57 Street (581-2760))
Pipino-Buccheri, 14 East 55 Street (759-2959)

▶ RICHARD STEIN
1018 LEXINGTON AVENUE (BETWEEN 72 AND 73 STREETS) (879-3663)

Unlike most of the salons who need you for their training sessions, this one is genuinely interested in establishing a permanent relationship with you. Unlike the usual cattle call, where you may or may not be chosen as a model, here *you* call up and make an appointment. Evening sessions are held every Tuesday for a cut, conditioning, and blow dry. These services are free, but tips are appreciated. The same services are available during the day, also by appointment—at times when the salon is not at its busiest—for a modest $18. You will be the client of a junior stylist, a licensed hairdresser who has already had some training in Richard Stein's method but still works under his supervision. The object here is to help the stylist gain his or her own following. It is hoped that you will come back regularly, free in the evening or cheaply during the day. After six months to a year, your stylist's fee will be raised to $30 and eventually to $45, the regular fee here. If that's more than you care to spend, you can start all over with another new talent.

Here you will be very welcome, even if your hair is too thin, too short, or not in the very best condition, because you will be a client, not a styling model. Most clients are not perfect, and your flaws will be considered a challenge. The junior stylists work hard to please, Richard Stein checks the final result every time, and the atmosphere is very pleasant—no loud rock music or abrasive trendiness.

OTHER BEAUTY SERVICES

▶ CHRISTINE VALMY INTERNATIONAL SCHOOL FOR AESTHETICS
260 FIFTH AVENUE
(581-1520)

In an elegant salon setting, very hushed and peaceful, you get an hour-long facial that leaves your skin very clean, stimulated, and fresh. The process involves cleaning, toning, and nourishing, and includes machines that gently cover your face with aromatic steam and an expert facial massage. Blackheads will be dealt with. Additional services may be suggested, like a vegetable peel to remove dead cells, or special masks to supplement the standard facial, which could cost in the neighborhood of $20. Your operator will be a student shortly before graduation, always supervised by a licensed cosmetologist. Mine was Japanese, all set to open her own salon in Tokyo.

The price for the facial is $20, or $15 with purchase of at least one Valmy product. An appointment is necessary.

A makeup consultation for day or evening makeup is $10 with purchase of at least one product.

The first time I had a facial at the school, a long time ago, there was real pressure to buy products, and I was given a tray with lots of products to try after my facial. The next time, years later, there was no product in sight and nobody even suggested using one. Prices and available procedures also change from time to time—

they used to do leg waxing, now they don't; when you read this, things may have changed again, but it's still a good place to have your face pampered.

9–7 M, W, 9–5 Tu, Th, F. Minimum for credit cards or checks, $50.

► S W E D I S H   I N S T I T U T E
226 WEST 26 STREET
(924-0991)

This serious, federally-accredited training institute for massage therapy is not at all like some of the massage parlors around town. Here you must bring a massage prescription from a physician, chiropractor, or dentist, stating either specific medical conditions or such things as back pain, job related tension, anxiety, stiff neck, or grinding of teeth. You are then evaluated and given half-hour massages once a week for seven consecutive weeks for a fee of $70. Both Swedish and shiatsu massage are available. Your masseur or masseuse will be a senior student who is fully trained and learning to work with different conditions; he or she will be closely supervised by an instructor.

S W I M M I N G ,   R U N N I N G
T R A C K S ,   W E I G H T   R O O M S ,
A N D   A E R O B I C S   C L A S S E S

Health clubs around town will promise you "discounts" from inflated membership dues and deliver crowded classes and locker rooms. Consider instead the very basic but free facilities offered by the recreation program of the New York City Parks Department. There are several facilities in Manhattan. They all provide lockers and showers, but you must bring your own towel, soap, and padlock.

▶ PARKS DEPARTMENT POOL AND GYM
342 EAST 54 STREET
(397-3154)

You need an ID card to get into the building and you must come in person to apply for it and pay a $2 fee.

Weekly aerobics classes cost $30 a semester. If you want to attend more than once a week, you pay $30 per semester for every weekday class. There is no fee for using the indoor running track, the gym with free weights, and a Universal machine, the large pool, or the basketball court, where players form casual teams and play together from 3–7 M, T, or W. At other times the court is used by youth groups or organized teams.

There is no wall-to-wall carpeting or soft lighting, but the place is clean and provides lockers and showers. Bring your own padlock, soap, and towel.

▶ PARKS DEPARTMENT POOL AND GYM
533 WEST 59 STREET
(397-3166)

Similar to the facility above, but there are no aerobics classes. For mountaineers-in-training there is a ceramic climbing wall that simulates rock-climbing conditions. There is also a Universal weight room, pool, and basketball court. To get your ID card, see Mr. Angelo Lawson 3–7 M–F.

▶ PARKS DEPARTMENT CARMINE STREET POOL AND GYM
3 CLARKSON STREET
(397-3107)

This Greenwich Village facility offers a pool, aerobics classes, a running track, basketball and volleyball courts, and a well-equipped Nautilus workout room. At the time of this writing, the only thing you pay is $1 for the ID card.

Apply for it 6–8 M–Th and bring a passport picture. By the time you read this, there will be a modest charge for using the facilities. The only drawback is, not surprisingly, this place is always crowded.

If you prefer to work out in the privacy of your home, you can buy or rent all sorts of exercise equipment at:

▶ BETTER HEALTH
5201 NEW UTRECHT AVENUE, BROOKLYN
(718-436-4801)

The company sells quality bicycles, rowing machines, treadmills, cross-country ski simulators, climbers, and other workout equipment at prices that are claimed to be 15 to 25 percent below retail. Brands include Trotter, Lifecycle, Marcy, Tunturi, Bodyguard, Vectra, Cal Gym, Powerstep, Altero, Universal, and others. They also sell and install saunas, steam showers, and hot tubs. They will deliver, install, and, if necessary, assemble the exercise equipment.

What's for sale can also be rented by the month, so you can try things out and see if you will stick to an exercise program at home. If all you need is some ankle weights and barbells, you can get them here at a discount.

The hours are M, Tu, W, 10–6, Th 10–8, Su 12–5, closed Friday and Saturday. Major credit cards are accepted. Returns accepted up to seven days for exchange, credit, or refund.

If you have a prescription for eyeglasses, you can take it to:

▶ UNIQUE EYEWEAR
19 WEST 34 STREET
(947-4977)

A tremendous selection of frames and every kind and color of lens, as well as very low prices compensate for the crowded, harried atmosphere and minimal service here. But your glasses will be carefully made and fitted, and that's what matters most.

Open 9–5 M–F, 9–6 Th, 10–2:30 Sa. Credit cards not accepted. Personal checks welcome.

If you want to order your glasses on Sunday in a less hectic atmosphere, go to:

► T R I A N G L E   O P T I C S
95 DELANCEY STREET
(674-3748)

Family-owned for several generations, this is a gentle place with attentive service. There is also an optometrist. Prices for reading glasses start at $15.

Open 9:30–5 six days a week, 10–5 Sa.

THRIFT AND
RESALE SHOPS

In your own home town you may never have considered digging in a charity thrift shop through the things other people no longer want. In New York you may miss a good bet if you don't. Think of all the celebrities who, after they have been photographed for the newspapers in an outfit, will never wear it in public again, because the photographers want to see them in something new the next time. Where does that almost-new outfit go? Often to a thrift shop, where you can pick it up for pin money. Think of all the furnishings that become obsolete because of a move or a change of taste or fashion. Do they go to the attic, to await another change of taste, a grown child's new home, an auction? Who's got an attic in this city? They go to a thrift shop, for a tax deduction. But not everything in the thrift shops is used. Even the most exclusive manufacturers and retailers give tons of brand-new things to charity—what else can they do with unsold merchandise? The thrift shops don't have much storage space and must turn donations over fast, so they price their wares to sell. With patience and perseverance one can furnish a whole apartment or assemble a whole wardrobe, complete with fur coat and evening gowns, in New York thrift shops. The less dedicated just stop in from time to time, cash in hand, to treasure hunt. A compulsive shopper can indulge herself wildly, and still be able to pay her bills—try that at Bendel's or Bergdorf's!

At these thrift shops some items may seem overpriced, while others are irresistible bargains. Remember that most of the pricing is done by volunteers who use their best judgment, which may not agree with your own. The thrill comes when you find the new, silk-lined kid gloves for $6, the signature scarf for $5, the good blue fox coat for $400, the $3 silk lampshade with the soiled spot that responds to a bit of cleaning fluid.

Many thrift shops accept credit cards for a minimum purchase of $20–$25; in others it's strictly cash. The more upscale shops have designer rooms for their best fashions and some require an appointment for shopping. There . . . how is that for class?

WHERE TO LOOK:

St. Luke's, 487 Hudson Street (Christopher Street) (924-9364)

Greenwich House, 27 Barrow Street (242-4140)

Hadassah, 231 Eighth Avenue (21st Street) (727-8977) Open Sunday.

Repeat Performance, 220 East 23 Street (684-5344)

Second Time Around, 220 East 23 Street (685-2170)

Everybody's Thrift Shop, 261 Park Avenue South (at 20th Street) (355-9263)

St. George's, 277 Park Avenue South (at 20th Street) (355-9263) For furniture.

St. George's, 61 Gramercy Park North (260-0350) Better merchandise.

St. George's, 209 East 16 Street (475-5510) This has the best prices of the three.

Helpline Thrift Shop, 383 Third Avenue (at 27th Street) (532-5136)

Postgraduate Center, 120 East 28 Street (683-3070)

Search and Save, 55 West 39 Street (988-1320)

St. Bartholomew's, Park Avenue at 51 Street (751-1616)

Return Engagement, 900 First Avenue (51st Street) (752-2679)

Council, 767 Ninth Avenue (between 51st and 52nd streets) (757-6132) Open Sunday.

New York Hospital, 439 East 71 Street (535-0965)

Arthritis Foundation, 121 East 77 Street (772-8816)

Girls' Club, 202 East 77 Street (535-8570)

Irvington House, 1534 Second Avenue (at 80th Street) (879-4555) Designer room by appointment.

Stuyvesant Square, 1704 Second Avenue (at 88th Street) (831-1830) Designer room.

Spence Chapin, 1430 Third Avenue (at 81st Street) (737-8448) Designer room.

Memorial Sloan Kettering, 1440 Third Avenue (at 81st Street) (535-1250) Designer room.

Cancer Care, 1480 Third Avenue (at 83rd Street) Designer room by appointment.

Thrift Shop East, 336 East 86 Street (772-6868)

The Harlem Restoration Project, 461 West 125 Street (864-6992)

Both Goodwill Industries and the Salvation Army operate a chain of thrift shops:

► GOODWILL INDUSTRIES:

186 Second Avenue (11th Street) (533-2768)

402 Third Avenue (29th Street) (679-0786)

1704 Second Avenue (88th Street) (831-1830)

130 West 3 Street (Sixth Ave) (673-0231)

201 Eighth Avenue (20th Street) (675-1520)

217 West 79 Street (874-5050)

730 Amsterdam Avenue (95th Street) (666-3655)

2196 Fifth Avenue (135th Street) (862-0020)

96-11 57 Avenue (Lefrak City) (718-592-9120)

4-21 27 Avenue, Astoria (718-728-5400)

▶ SALVATION ARMY

112 Fourth Avenue (12th Street) (673-2741)
40 Avenue B (3rd Street) (473-9492)
220 East 23 Street (532-8115)
208 Eighth Avenue (20th Street) (929-5214)
536 West 46 Street (757-2311) The flagship store.
268 West 96 Street (663-2258)
39-11 61 Street, Woodside (718-426-9222)
34-02 Steinway Street, Astoria (718-784-9880)

RESALE SHOPS

In addition to thrift shops run by charities, there are some very upscale resale shops. They are second-hand clothing stores of a special kind: they carry only the very best, in excellent condition. Jackie Onassis sent clothes from the White House to such a store. I know one very well-dressed editor with an unusual figure, who found that a European aristocrat with an identical figure sells her hardly worn French couture to a resale shop. The shop calls my friend when the baroness sends something and it fits her perfectly.

Prices in resale shops may be a little higher than those in charity shops. After all, these shops pay for their merchandise and their salesladies are not volunteers.

There are rich men who gladly pay their wives' extravagant clothing bills but keep them very short of cash. What's a girl to do? She buys clothes and sells them for cash in a resale shop. Recently a Galanos beaded jacket, unworn with the $9990 price tag in place, came into a resale shop, where it sold, quickly, for $550. More usually, the prices are about one-third of the original price or less, when the clothes originally cost $200–$500.

▶ EXCHANGE UNLIMITED
563 SECOND AVENUE (31ST STREET)
(889-3229)

The only resale shop that also has men's fashions. *Open 12–7 M–Sa*. No credit cards. All sales final. Prices approximately one-third of original cost, less on very expensive items.

▶ ENCORE
1132 MADISON AVENUE (84TH STREET)
(879-2850)

Open 10:30–6 M–Sa, till 8 Th, 12:30–6 Su. Closed Sundays in summer. No credit cards. All sales final.

▶ MICHAEL'S
1041 MADISON AVENUE (79TH ST.)
(737-7273)

Open 9:30–6 M–Sa, till 8 on Th. Visa and MasterCard accepted. All sales final. Prices one-third of original cost, less on very expensive items.

Children's clothes can be outgrown before they were worn, or very soon thereafter. These two stores specialize in children's resale. Their merchandise is always in excellent condition and is sold at approximately half the original cost, or less.

▶ SECOND ACT
1046 MADISON AVENUE
(988-2440)

Open 9–5 T–Sat. Credit cards not accepted, checks welcome. All sales final.

► SECOND COUSIN

142 SEVENTH AVENUE (10TH STREET)

(929-8048)

11–7 M–Sa. Major credit cards are accepted. All sales final on resale items. The store also carries new merchandise.

SEE ALSO:

Second Cousin in Chapter 14.

SERVICES

HARD-TO-FIND SPECIALISTS

You paid hundreds, perhaps thousands for your hi-fi components or computer, but when you need repairs, where do you find someone who will do it well and honestly? It's often a problem. A really knowledgeable person can probably find a better job than working for a repair service, but if such a person moonlights on his own time, you want his address:

COMPUTER REPAIR AND CONSULTATION

If you are new to personal computers, you might want to discuss your requirements with an independent consultant before you buy. He or she can give you more time than most retailers, and can also help you install your system and get started on it.

Someone I know was ready to buy a computer, monitor, printer, software and accessories, as recommended by a retailer. Then she checked with:

► RICHARD JAGOW
(340-6561) OR (674-0533)

who works as a medical computer specialist during the day and moonlights as a hardware repair person and consultant. Not only did Jagow change my friend's shopping list to something better suited to her needs, what he recommended cost over a thousand dollars less than the store's recommendation. After she bought her computer, he set it up and helped install the software.

Jagow has made housecalls to my computer during some chilling moments when it would not respond, and has always saved the day when the power supply needed replacing and on a few occasions when only a cord had become undone or a diskette forgotten in the drive, sending me into a panic. I was glad to pay for the visit, because it saved untold anxiety and because his prices are really reasonable.

HOME ELECTRONICS REPAIR

► ANTONIOS
(861-8665)

is in charge of maintaining the communications equipment at the U.N. On his own time he makes housecalls to sick hi-fi and TV sets, VCRs, and other home electronics. He is not only superbly skillful, he is totally honest and would not dream of selling you a part you don't need. His fees are also reasonable.

UPHOLSTERY AND DRAPERY WORKROOMS

Buy your fabric at one of the good resources in chapter 18 and have your re-upholstery, slipcovers, or draperies done at a workroom, where you pay only for labor. Good craftsmanship is never cheap, but the total job will cost less and you will get excellent work from one of the following:

▶ V A N   D A M   U P H O L S T E R Y
3414 CHURCH AVENUE, BROOKLYN
(718-469-7216)

Nice service, impeccable workmanship, and good prices distinguish this firm of European craftsmen, who also have a branch in Belgium. They do both upholstery and drapery work.

▶ L O R E   D E C O R A T O R S
2201 THIRD AVENUE
(534-1025)

These people are contractors for many of the shops that offer custom work to those who purchase fabric from them. They do a large volume of work for these clients and charge appropriately low prices. As a private customer, you may at first be quoted a price that is really just a basis for negotiation, so try to negotiate. Their work on upholstery is excellent. They sub-contract drapery work, so you are better off dealing directly with the people who do the work.

SEE ALSO:

Forsyth Decorators in the Grand Street Walking Tour.

ALTERATIONS

When your clothes need altering, you want a tailor you can trust. The following will do good work and charge accordingly—there are no discounts on skilled labor:

▶ P E P P I N O

780 LEXINGTON AVENUE (BETWEEN 60TH AND 61ST
STREETS)
(832-3844)

Peppino and his people do not only wield a fine needle, he has a
sure sense of style and proportion and is used to working on
expensive clothes of all kinds, from men's suits to winter coats to
chiffon dresses. The first time I brought him a coat to shorten, he
declared the length perfect and refused to touch it, and he was
absolutely right. Shortening that coat would have ruined it. *His
hours are 9–6:30 M–F, 9–4 Sa.* Cash and checks only.

▶ M A R S A N   T A I L O R S   I N   T H E
S A I N T   L A U R I E   B U I L D I N G

899 BROADWAY (20TH STREET)
(475-2727)

These tailors do the free alterations on Saint Laurie's suits and
coats, but they will work on any tailored garment you bring in, for
a fee, and they do excellent work.
The hours are 9:30–5:30 M–F, 9:30–7 Th, 9:30–5 Sa, 12–4 Su.

▶ F L O R M O N T   T A I L O R

857 BROADWAY (17TH STREET)
(255-2549)

Another reliable shop which can be trusted with your good clothes.
The hours are 7:30–4 M–F, 7:30–9 Th.

INDEX